# CHART A COURSE

D1316410

# CHART

# A

# COURSE

TAKING A JOURNEY
WITH GOD AT THE HELM

*J. CAREY*

Chart A Course by Jessica Carey
Published by Carey Media LLC Queen Creek, AZ 85142

www.jessicacarey.co

© 2019 Jessica Carey

All rights reserved. No portion of this book may be reproduced in any form without permission
from the publisher, except as permitted by U.S. copyright law. For permissions contact:

info@jessicacarey.co

Cover and design by Erik Peterson.

Back Cover Photo credit Jordan Darby.

ISBN: 978-0-578-22565-4

# TABLE OF CONTENTS

"Who am I, and where am I going?" These two fundamental questions are asked by everyone traveling through life, and because they are so universally basic, accurate answers are essential to the outcome of our journey.

*Chart A Course* is a book full of these essentials. It is a manual for navigating life, providing clear insights, practical examples, and relevant warnings to help the traveller survive the journey and actually get somewhere in life. By sharing many of her own hard-fought experiences, Jessica Carey takes us along a course that is readily understandable, easily duplicated, and thoroughly tested. Her examples are honest. Her conclusions are sound. The guidance she offers is not based on opinion or cultural norms, but rather on the timeless map offered in the Word of God. This is a trustworthy map full of simple, powerful truths that apply to everyone seeking to walk in heaven's harmony on their own journey through life.

I have seen Jessica sail through many storms, watched her wrestle with the wind and the waves, and prayed with and for her through many of the seasons she describes. And I can say with great assurance that if you will read this book thoughtfully and apply these principles with faith in the God who made you, your journey to that heavenly shore will not only be successful but will enable others to arrive safely as well.

There is never a need to wonder or wander through life. There is a Chart for your Course. Let this book help you discover yours.

Nori Chesney
Global Missionary
London, England

## AUTHOR'S NOTE

C hart a course.

Those were the words echoing through my head as I watched a beautiful promotional video at a women's conference I attend almost every year called "Colour." The theme of the conference was "The Wind in Her Sails." The video showed images of big rolling waves and a gorgeous ship with full sails that seemed to promise adventure. However, there was a voice inside my head nudging me; this was only part of the picture. The voice was one I had grown familiar with during my own journey: it was the Holy Spirit. The phrase "chart a course" stuck in my mind and was followed quickly by the thought: all the wind in your sails don't matter one bit if you didn't chart a course.

In that moment I didn't fully understand what it meant, but I was curious enough to investigate further.

What does it mean to chart a course? In navigational terms I found it was defined as: "To plan a direction of travel by using a chart and taking into consideration all the variables such as the speed of the boat, winds, currents, tides, water depth, hazards, markers and time."[1]

In other words, charting a course means making plans to arrive at a selected destination. I questioned why God had impressed this phrase on me? I think I am pretty good at planning. At least these days, I am. I wasn't always a planner.

As a young adult while living in New York City, I was at the mercy of the winds and waves of my life. I didn't make plans to arrive anywhere and I believed that fate or destiny would eventually lead me to where I was supposed to go. This resigned attitude to let the "universe" decide where I would end up did not ultimately lead to what I felt were my deepest desires. I wanted to belong. I wanted to feel accepted. I wanted to have genuine relationships. However, my journey was more like a spilled glass of water running along the path of least resistance to a huge drop off over a dangerous cliff.

In my personal life, and my spiritual life, I was like a ship tossed at sea, with no clue as to which way would lead to fulfillment. The fulfillment I was chasing was inclusion, a sense of belonging and a life lived with purpose. I hungered to have deep and unshakable self confidence. I moved to New York City to pursue my dream of becoming an actress, in hopes to find fulfillment, but that didn't do it. I attended one of the best universities for theater arts, but that didn't do it. I auditioned like a crazy woman, but that didn't do it. I booked jobs and premiered as the lead in an off-off-broadway show, but that didn't do it. I was in and out of relationships with powerful men, with rich men, and with other poor actors and again, I felt depleted.

I longed to be known and loved and adored, but all I really found was a shallow, selfish world. A world where I was the self-absorbed star in my own drama. I was constantly changing my ideals and my persona in an effort to gain the accolades of others. When I was with my "country-western" loving friends, I was as much a cowgirl as the next. When I got invited to the opera, I wore an elegant ball gown and adjusted my speech to be equally elegant. When I was hanging around other rejected actors I worked with, I lied about the level of interest or success that I was anticipating. I was confused, I was lost, and I was hurting.

I longed to be loved, but I hated who I was becoming. During this season of my life I knew I needed an anchor. Something that would help me to stay true to myself. Something that would inform my decisions in such a way to stay committed to my purpose. Something that helped me to know my own value, and to stop allowing others to belittle, abuse, ignore, and take advantage of me. It was in a moment of deep depression and being overwhelmed by a feeling of hopelessness that I cried out for help. I cried out to "God." I was unsure if God was available to me. I didn't know if He would answer. I doubted that my life and it's problems would be worth His attention.

I was wrong.

God did hear my voice. He did answer. His response was in the form of sending someone to speak a word of truth over my life. The person God sent was a beautiful faith-filled woman who asked me a simple question: "Do you want to keep doing things your way, or try them God's way?"

"Well, I'm clearly flubbing it up! I might as well try it His way," I retorted. Although at the time, I didn't say flubbing.

It was in that moment of honesty and desperation that God stepped into my boat and assumed control of the helm. He knew the precise direction to choose in order to realign my life. I didn't come to realize the full freedom of this shift until almost eight months later, when I passionately surrendered my whole life to serving God and His purposes. From that moment, I started learning how to hear the voice of my Creator and follow His instructions. I have discovered over time how to carefully chart a course with God at the helm. It has been a wild journey but well worth the risk.

# Introduction
# to Chart a Course

C*hart a Course* juxtaposes the techniques of ancient sea navigation with our modern day spiritual navigation. It explores the analogy of sailing the seas according to the unmoving celestial bodies of the stars and sky, in tandem to pursuing our spiritual journey according to the guidance of the Creator of those celestial bodies.

The process of charting a course is not a once in a lifetime activity. It is an ongoing practice of planning for what lies ahead. It is preparing and being present, it is persevering through the challenging parts of our adventure. It is the willingness to continually sharpen our skills to discern the leading of God, and remain flexible in the times we must wait. I have spent the last decade learning how to navigate according to God's design. I have tried many strategies; some have failed and some have succeeded. I have felt unstoppable when I get a vision of the future, and then felt crushed when that vision was delayed or disrupted. During my journey I have experienced a great deal of what the seas offer to those that dare to pull up anchor and set sail.

I have prayed and wept, praised and leapt.

These experiences have grounded me more fully in my faith,

and also opened new horizons I thought were not available to someone like me. I have always wanted to become the kind of confident woman who seems unflappable. You know, the kind with that deep certainty about their destiny. I am still striving to become that woman, but my hope is that this book will encourage us to boldly follow the leading of God. With God as our captain, we will no doubt become more confident in the protection, guidance, and provision of Him who formed the seas!

How many times have you wanted to do something? Go somewhere? Or learn something new and never did? Were you afraid? Were you reluctant? Perhaps you have been burned in the past so rather than endure the possibility of pain again, you just stayed in the port called "comfort." Or maybe you were like me and feel like you are allowing life to float by, without having any intention to go in a particular way. Perhaps you are finding yourself adrift among the circumstances life has presented?

I hope to encourage you to dream again, to tap into your divine calling, and to prepare for a successful spiritual adventure. I will share personal testimonies and strategies of how to persevere through the storms of life. I will challenge you to select a strong crew that you will lean on throughout your journey. I will present questions that will help you gain the courage to pull up the anchor of reluctance and set sail for new uncharted waters.

God-sized dreams have the potential to paralyze us and simultaneously stretch us into the person we were always meant to become. I don't want any of us to encounter circumstances that cause us to lose momentum or stop pursuing our dreams altogether. If you have attempted a dream and it fizzled out, it can be painfully discouraging. It can destroy our ability to be effective in impacting our world. It can cast a negative shadow on our future endeavors by reinforcing our inadequacies or insecurities. Taking a journey can invigorate us, intimidate us, and test our mettle in the best possible way.

*Chart a Course* outlines how I hope to approach my future: with the best laid plans, and the fearless faith that God knows exactly what I will encounter and how He will pull me through every obstacle.

> **Proverbs 3:5-6 / Trust in the Lord with all your heart and lean not on your own understanding; in all your ways submit to Him, and He will make your paths straight. (NIV)**[1]

If you are ready to fearlessly face your future, and you desire God to be the guiding force, let's begin to chart your course. How? We start with the map.

# Section 1

## The Basics of Charting a Course

### CHAPTER 1

# Consult the Map

The first step when we embark on a journey requires looking at a navigational chart, or simply put, a map. There are many details on a nautical map including distances, directions, a compass rose, and the topography (ports, landmarks, natural and cultural features) as well as the hydrography (tides, currents, depths, rocks, wrecks, obstructions, common routes).[1] The best way to start planning a journey is with a good map. The more the map can outline what the journey might look like, the better chance you have of arriving safely. Now, I don't think many of you are planning on sailing around the world, but I am guessing many of you would like to go where you feel God is leading.

Start with your map, which is the word of God. The Bible is always where we begin to uncover the unique course we are to take in life. God made no mistakes in how He created the Bible: He started very perfectly, "In the Beginning…" Check out Genesis:1-2, where God's story begins with how he designed us to live. Adam and Eve were created to be in constant communion with God the Father. They had daily conversations, dinners, workouts, and snuggles with their Creator. Doesn't that sound nice? Just being able to lay your head on the chest of the Creator of the universe and tell Him how great you think the pineapple you are eating is? That is what God intended. Okay, I'm not totally sure about the cuddling, but I am confident He desires to be in constant communion with His creation.

Through His word, God inspired, authored, and designed every subsequent story, poem, historical account, and gospel to lead us back to divine communion with our Maker.

Each journey will be different; for example, maybe you are launching a new business and you need wisdom. There are several books that will dive into what it means to have Biblical wisdom including; Job, Psalms, Proverbs and Ecclesiastes. What if you desire a godly spouse? Check out the love poem in the Song of Songs. Or perhaps you need healing? There are many stories of miraculous recoveries in the Gospels found in the books of Matthew, Mark, Luke, and John. Regardless of what your journey might contain, every problem or situation that you encounter has an answer in the Word of God. God created a beautiful map back to Himself, and He will use your journey, your desires, and your unique talents to bring you into a deeper relationship with Him.

I have found that at varying intervals in my life God's word would reveal different things to me. It functioned like a living map; as I moved and went through different seasons, the map helped me to navigate accordingly.

**Hebrews 4:12 / For the word of God is alive and active. Sharper than any double-edged sword, it penetrates even to dividing soul and spirit, joints and marrow; it judges thoughts and attitudes of the heart. (NIV)**

When I was newly married and I worried about my husband, Alex, there were passages that spoke to me about how to respect, trust, and honor my spouse. A bit later when I became a mom and I worried about my children, Kennedy and Truman, there were passages that talked about love and correction. Then a bit further down the road, when I became a business owner and I worried about everything, I was shown how to build faith in God for finances, wisdom, and forgiveness. In each season, I made a habit of consulting the map to see what God advised. Each time was different, because I was effectively looking at a different map. The Bible is like a collection of maps. There is a scripture, story, parable, analogy or song that will be precisely what you need to navigate well through every part of your journey. God will reveal the particular Bible segment that will speak to you.

The word of God is a living guidebook, in constant motion, even if we cannot perceive it. Similar to a seed planted in the earth, our human eyes are not able to visibly see the growth and the violent expansion of the seed as it develops, but it is growing, moving, and expanding nonetheless. This observation of nature helps me to understand the concept of the living word; that while I am not always able to perceive how my study of the Bible is impacting me, it is still guiding, protecting, influencing, and helping me to grow. This is why I leverage this tool as my map for life. As you journey and begin to consult the map more often you will start to read it with more clarity and understanding. You will grow in your skill of reading the map, and perceiving what will be required of you during the journey.

### CHAPTER 2

# Developing into a Senior Navigator

When I first started reading the Bible I was like a junior navigator. I obviously could read but I wasn't able to create a well thought-out plan based on my limited understanding. I often played "Bible Roulette" in an effort to find direction. When I was struggling with some situation or was looking for an answer, I would randomly turn to a page for an answer from God. If I was feeling depressed, I would flick the pages and land on a scripture. If it seemed out of context, I would flip again until I "felt" like I got the answer I was looking for. Fortunately, God is faithful even when we use His book as a fortune-telling tool. I found comfort and guidance in the words on the page. The only problem with this strategy long term is that it is not intentional. It is not really charting a course and creating a plan: it is searching in a library of self-help books for the one that tells you what you want to hear.

In order to chart well and fully utilize a map, you must know how to read the symbols, landmarks, and keys found on it. You must also know how to interpret the map in order to calculate real life distances, time, and possible resources that will be needed to get to your destination. Reading the Bible is similar in that to get the most out of it you need to understand how to read it, decipher meaning, and calculate real life applications. This skill is developed over time so don't be discouraged if you haven't read a single scripture. The point is to begin to uncover what the Bible has to show you. Regardless of whether you are a devout Bible reader, or have never picked one up, I can promise you that all of us benefit from a regular practice of reading God's word.

Practically speaking, the best place to start is to find a translation of the Bible that really speaks to you. There are hundreds of versions of the Bible and they all offer a unique "flavor" and readability. One of the more modern versions that is a paraphrase, but very readable is *The Message* translation. I prefer the New King James Version (NKJV) or the New International Version (NIV). I grew up hearing and reading from them, plus I studied Elizabethan literature so the "THEES and THOUS" do not throw me off. The point is to try a few different translations until you find a favorite. Also, if you have a favorite already, maybe try a new version and see what perspective changes it might offer.

Once you find a comfortable translation, the next step is to find a story in the word that is of interest to you. Maybe you are interested in women's roles in the Bible, so start with the book of Ruth or the story of Queen Esther. If you are into battles, epic sagas, and the constant changing of power, feel free to start in the book of Kings. Use the power of the internet to help you narrow down where to start. For example, if you are struggling with abandonment, search for scriptures about being an adopted son or daughter of God. If you are dealing with a health concern, search for Jesus' miraculous healings. If you are worried about money, search for God's provision. You will no doubt get a large list of potential scriptures to start reading and learning.

A word of caution: oftentimes a single scripture passage taken out of context doesn't give you the full picture. It is like looking at a corner of the map but not seeing to the edge. Reading the scriptures before and after help to provide clarity about the intention and context of that passage. Do not get discouraged if you read back to the beginning of the chapter and you still feel lost. I have often read, and re-read, a scripture passage that I didn't understand and it wasn't until much later in my spiritual journey that I managed to glean some understanding from it. It takes time and experience to develop into a senior navigator, where you are more able to interpret what you are seeing.

Please do not feel pressured to read the whole Bible cover to cover right away. Build up to that task! However, I strongly recommend doing this at some point because it gives you a fuller understanding of the unchanging nature of God. The "Old Testament" God found in Genesis, Exodus, Daniel and much of the Old Testament is often perceived as a passionate, jealous, just, and all powerful God; the "fire and brimstone" kind of God. However, the God we meet as Jesus in the "New Testament" is humble, compassionate, loving, and revolutionary. Reading through the whole Bible will give more context to how these seemingly disparate portrayals are actually the same all encompassing Savior.

Another tactic to gain understanding from the word of God is to attend a Bible-based church where the word is spoken and taught from each week. There are so many gifted teachers and preachers of God's word that can enlighten us about scriptures. I encourage you to find one near you. If you have difficulty getting to a church each week, consider finding one that offers a televised version of their services. Developing into a senior navigator requires practice. It requires diligence to read the Word regularly even when we don't understand everything we may encounter. It requires a hunger to learn and to find resources that will help us understand.

### CHAPTER 3

# Drawing Course Lines

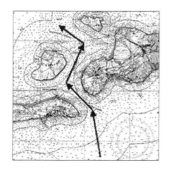

After finding a good map, the second step in manually charting and navigating is to draw a sequence of course lines. "Course lines are a line of position plotted on a chart, parallel to the intended course of a craft, showing whether the craft is to the left of its course."[1]

This might be a straight line from start to finish, or it could be a series of lines that navigate around landmarks, shallows, and hazards. Each course line will have a specific direction or heading and a starting and ending point. Course lines are what I will call "seasons" within the journey. They are chunks of the overall trip that are limited by many factors, but each will get you a bit closer to your final destination. Your course lines or seasons will be marked by different hurdles, timelines, and revelations.

If you take my personal dream of becoming a writer, then one of those course lines might be to partner with a great copy editor, or it could involve some networking events, additional financial resources, or both. It is a specific season of the journey that will no doubt bring you closer to the actual desired ending. With regards to our spiritual journey this could involve a season where you address unforgiveness, toxic relationships, disbelief, or loss and grief. When you first begin to plan stay focused on the initial course lines of the journey. These are the first steps you would take. If you want to become a teacher it might require additional schooling. If you feel called to preach you might need to spend time practicing public speaking. The destination will determine the direction, and the specific directives. Keep in mind that as you begin to move, those lines are liable to change and shift. As you learn more about where you are going, you will discover more course lines that will need to be added to your chart. Prayerfully consider drafting a list of these lines, which might resemble a step by step process to get to your desired destination.

I recently experienced a pretty terrifying health scare when I was awakened in the middle of the night by intense chest pain. The episode only lasted about twenty minutes and I attributed it to heart burn, even though I had rarely suffered from it. When I woke up, I called my sister who is a nurse that works in a catheterization lab, also known as a cath lab. It is a diagnostic clinic where they visualize the internal arteries and chambers of the heart. She works with cardiac patients everyday so I just thought I'd run my little episode by her to give myself peace of mind. She told me to immediately start a low-dose adult aspirin regimen until I could get in to see someone. My sister, Michelle, is not prone to freaking out, medically speaking, so when she gave me this advice I started to panic. I felt fear grab a hold of my innermost being and shake it furiously.

Later that same week, I ended up in the emergency room.

I had been an athlete from the age of 12, so this was not supposed to happen to me. I jokingly told Alex I was upset my body was betraying me. I told him, "I treat this body like a Porsche and it's breaking down like a Pinto." Humor is one of my greatest coping mechanisms. I highly recommend it in intense situations!

I had quickly come about around a peninsula and entered another season of life. This new region of illness was completely foreign to me. My ship was suddenly in a new territory, and I wasn't prepared. I needed to put a plan in place so that I was able to trust God during this segment of my journey. I consulted the map. I began to research in the Bible for how to address sickness and disease. From my research I created an initial set of course lines.

1. Contact primary care physician
2. Call the "elders" of the church to pray for me
3. Thank God.
4. Pray for healing and insight into what is going on with my body
5. Reflect on stressors in my life and my schedule
6. Pray before attending each and every doctor visit
7. Read what the Word has to say about healing
8. Trust God, trust God, trust God
9. Follow Doctor recommendations
10. Repeat as necessary

Even in the first few weeks of my infirmity, God revealed some major truths about my life. He showed me that when my health was threatened, I didn't run to the arms of the Great Physician. I got scared, I panicked, and I immediately began thinking of all the things "I" should do to get better. In that moment of terror I took hold of the captain's wheel, instead of trusting God. I was trying to change my circumstances in my own strength. Navigating a "health hurricane" without God making all of the decisions is NOT recommended.

In addition to the revelation of my fears, God showed me that I harbored some judgmental tendencies toward people that appear to make unhealthy choices. I have several people in my family who suffer with diabetes but they eat high fat and high sugar foods almost everyday. I had a neighbor who was hooked up to oxygen but he smoked like a chimney. In my opinion these "choices" caused a self-inflicted illness. The Lord chastised my thinking by allowing me to experience symptoms that based on my life choices, I should have been able to avoid.

It was humbling to be able to run four miles one day and barely able to walk up the stairs the next. The message was clear: just because we make mistakes, it does not mean we deserve to be sick. God didn't intend for us to live a life of infirmity.

Lastly, he revealed a gap in my faith to believe for a miraculous healing. I was really good at praying and believing for God's goodness and mercy in other people's lives. For example, just before my own health crisis I boldly prayed along with a group of believers for a friend of mine. She was told there was no way she would give birth to a living, healthy son after her amniotic fluid drained midway through her pregnancy. She was told it was virtually impossible for it to return on it's own. The doctors told her to expect to deliver a stillborn. I got on my knees and fully trusted my beautiful Creator with that baby's life. I prayed and believed with her, and I wasn't surprised when the amniotic fluid returned and she gave birth to a gorgeous boy a few months later.

However, I realized there was a doubt in believing for that same kind of restoration in my own body. My wonderful savior doesn't want me to lack any good thing. Total faith in Him is at the top of the list! I was graciously shown where I needed to stretch, learn, and trust. The season I was navigating was illness, but the destination I was navigating toward included increased faith, humility, and healing.

Each season, or course in our journey, will have hidden treasure waiting for us to discover. As you prayerfully consider your destination, create a course line list which will serve as a reminder of how to navigate during that particular season and be on the lookout for the hidden treasure along the way.

### CHAPTER 4

# Tools for Navigation

For the purposes of establishing a strong picture of navigating with God as our captain, I wanted to illustrate some connections between the tools used by ancient seafarers and the triune nature of God. For me, taking a sea voyage feels ancient and romantic, and this type of eternal love and grandeur is paralleled in the essence of God presented through the scriptures. As a Christian I believe in God as a singular entity with three distinct persons: God the Father, God the Son, and God the Holy Spirit. These three uniquely independent representations of God make up the singular trinity. I will not attempt to explain this in great detail, however there are several very well written books on this topic. Please humor me with the following analogies.

### The Compass

I am sure most of you are familiar with the purpose of a compass, which is to point north. It was used by ancient sailors to determine the direction they were traveling. A compass functions because any magnetized object that is allowed to spin freely will always point toward magnetic north.

From the beginning of time when God created the Earth, He built in an invisible global magnetic tracking system. God knew that our surroundings, our circumstances, and our emotions would not always tell us which way to go. He knew we would need something to give us directions back home. God knew we would need help finding our way, because it is easy to get lost. Life can spin out in such a way that we are unable to determine the best direction.

What points in the same direction consistently in our walk of faith? I would say, Jesus always points us toward communion with Himself and God the Father. His entire life points to His submission and love toward our Heavenly Father. Every story of healing, redemption, restoration, sovereignty, and salvation bows to the glory, power, and love of God. When Jesus was tempted, He relied on God's word to resist it. When His friend Lazarus died of an illness, He grieved and then prayed to His Father to resurrect him. When He was called to do the most difficult thing in His life, to go to the cross, He asked for the cup to pass over Him. In the end He trusted the Father's will, not His own.

If you are unsure of which direction to go, look to Jesus. Through the scriptures Jesus will reveal how to proceed, how to live your life according to God's will. How this actually happens will be unique to each individual.

I know it is cliche but asking yourself "What would Jesus Do?" is kind of like looking at a compass and seeing if you are headed in the right direction. If you sense that you are not doing what Jesus would do, those are clues that you might have drifted off course.

Those "aha" moments are just like looking at a compass that tells you which way is north.

**John 14:6 / Jesus answered, "I am the way and the truth and the life. No one comes to the Father except through me." (NIV)**

A quick example of how I had to look at my compass happened when someone told my husband he was an irresponsible person and a poor father. My "mama bear" instinct went full throttle after the brazen tongue lashing. In my head, I thought, "Who do they think they are?" I could have easily pointed out twenty things this person had done that would clearly put them in the irresponsible camp. I held a grudge for a little bit, but eventually I looked at Jesus and knew I had to let go of my offense. Jesus was wrongly accused, condemned, and put to death, and yet He showed us grace and forgiveness. If I wanted to truly lead the life I was called to I had to forgive.

Alex is a great man of God, a fabulous father, and one of the most generous people I know. It was so hard to see him hurting because of someone's careless words. The following scripture helped me to recalibrate:

**Luke 23:34 / Jesus said, "Father forgive them, for they do not know what they are doing." (NIV)**

Jesus was pointing me in the direction of grace. Could I extend grace to someone who didn't realize how piercing their words would be to Alex? Yes, I could.

Jesus is our compass and He is faithful to point us in the right direction in every circumstance. I believe that when Jesus died on the cross He created an intersection point for all of us to be changed and empowered to choose a different path. Whatever you believe is causing you to veer off course, Christ conquered it and will bring about change in you to achieve His purposes. He is our compass, always pointing us toward a healthy and ongoing relationship with God. Just like a compass freely spins toward magnetic north, our surrendered soul will point us toward the life and likeness of Jesus.

### *The Compass Rose*

While a compass was used to find north, the compass rose was used to create a more accurate course. The compass rose denotes the cardinal directions: north, south, east, and west. It also determines the difference between true north and magnetic north.

Isn't north always north?

True north is the unchanging geographical location of converging longitude lines. It is always found in the middle of the Arctic Ocean. However, magnetic north shifts slightly every day depending on where you are in the world.

The compass points to magnetic north, not necessarily precisely at true north. All this to say that the compass rose on your map would show the specific magnetic fluctuation in that part of the world. For example the compass rose on a map of South Africa will be very different than one of North America. Without boring you with a lot of math, the point of the compass rose was accuracy. Sailors would make adjustments in their course bearings according to the details indicated on the compass rose.

How this relates to our spiritual journey is that God always was, is, and will be our unchanging True North. He is the key intersecting point of our lives regardless of the changing nature of our circumstances. No matter where you are or what you are experiencing, He is consistent.

A disclaimer I would like to point out is that Jesus doesn't have the same shortcomings as a compass; He always points directly to God. However, our circumstances can cause us to misinterpret the reading of the compass. This is why we need to tune into the Holy Spirit, our spiritual compass rose.

The Holy Spirit provides understanding about whether the choices we are making are leading us back to God or away from Him. Are we following the path or are we drifting off course? Accurate interpretation of the will of the Father requires not only looking to the life and legacy of Christ, but also dialing into the frequency of the Holy Spirit.

For our analogy, I equate the use of the compass rose to tuning into the leading of the Holy Spirit. Consulting the Holy Spirit helps us adjust our journey, our attitude, and our perspective to align with the will and plan of God the Father and Christ His Son. We more accurately navigate toward the plan God intended.

Jesus promises regarding the Holy Spirit:

**John 14:26 / But the Advocate, the Holy Spirit, whom the Father will send in My name, will teach you all things and remind you of everything I have said to you. (NIV)**

This is a promise that the Holy Spirit will teach us, guide us, and remind us of the testimony of Jesus.

As an example, you might have heard from God to serve in a care facility, but you are unsure of what type. You love kids, but you are not sure if you can handle a children's cancer hospital. You are being led, but the specific details are cloudy. Specifics are the specialty of the Holy Spirit.

He was sent by God the Father, to guide us to the specific places and circumstances that bring fullness to our lives. In the case of the care facility, you may sense that you should work with mentally handicapped children. It just so happens there is a facility in your neighborhood. You take a step to call to inquire about volunteering and the receptionist is someone you went to college with. The tiny adjustments to the plan come from the guidance and empowerment of the Holy Spirit.

The compass rose indicates the directions and the differences in course bearings sailors would need to make in that particular part of the world. Similarly the Holy Spirit will indicate the directions and the adjustments we might need to make during our own journey in order to stay on course. If you are totally confused, I pray you will keep reading because I discuss more details about how to be sensitive to the voice of the Holy Spirit later in the book.

## *Jacob's Staff—A tool for the unknown*

As I studied tools used in ancient navigation I came across the Cross Staff, also known as Jacob's Staff. This antique tool was used to determine angles between the horizon and a fixed object, like the sun or stars. This would allow sailors to find their position in relation to these objects and other points that were visible on the map. The tool was made known by the Jewish Mathematician Levi Ben Gerson, in the 13th century when Europeans were needing to explore beyond the Mediterranean.[1]

There was a need and a desire to move beyond what was known. In order to facilitate this it was necessary to utilize the cross staff and make accurate calculations.

If you want to move beyond what is known and explore new horizons, make the cross of Christ your reference point in relation to everything else. The image below shows the way in which this

tool might have been used practically, placing the cross close to your eye and then calculating the distance between two points.[2]

In order for us as Christians to move ahead and make better plans, the cross of Christ must be in our vision. It must be what we focus on as we explore beyond our current ability. Practically speaking, making the cross of Christ your reference point is reflecting on the story of the death and resurrection of Jesus. You can find details of the story in all four gospels: Matthew, Mark, Luke, and John, as well as most books of the New Testament. Explore what this story means to you? What could it do in your life? What has it done already?

The story will not disappoint, as it tells of the sacrificial love of Jesus and His subsequent victory over all that stands in the way of our wholeness. When we place our vision in line with the cross, we see clearly how far off course we may have drifted. It also gives us a reference point to align ourselves with what God's plans are for our own personal victory.

If you have been a Christian for a long time, spend a moment reflecting back on the moment or period of life where you felt a releasing of the old life and embracing the new. If you are a new Christian or feel like a new Christian, consider what Jesus' sacrifice means to you.

When I have gone through dry spells in my spiritual journey and I have a longing to refresh the passion I felt when I first became a Christian, I think back to the moment where I gave my life to serve God. I remember how miserable I was living in New York, in a fruitless and loveless relationship, working long hours as a waitress and trying to make it as an actress. I was prostituting myself to the world in hopes someone would see something of value in me. I was willing to do almost anything to remove the fear of worthlessness that continued to haunt me.

Thinking back on the moment when I decided to let God take the helm makes me chuckle because as soon as I got out of the way and let God take control, my life changed rapidly. Once I started to dig into what Jesus did for me, I was overwhelmed with a feeling of deep gratitude. I could hardly believe that a person I never met, I could never repay, and I couldn't glorify while He was on Earth, was willing to sacrifice His life for me. I knew the story of Christ, but I didn't KNOW Him in my spirit. I didn't feel the love that Jesus poured out when He went to the cross and declared, "It is finished!"

As I learned these things I saw the moment when I decided to give God a try as the moment where, deep down, my insecurities started dying. I began seeing in myself more of the woman He had created me to be. Keeping this story in the center of my heart helps me to see God still working consistently in my life.

No matter whether you let Jesus take the helm of your ship a long time ago, it is important to circle back to the story of His death and resurrection. It helps us to build up the courage to explore new seas.

Just like Jacob's Staff helped sailors move into the unknown, the cross of Christ will give you the courage, confidence and passion to move into your own unknown. If you feel adrift, or you are not sure how to move forward, I recommend framing your situation with the cross at the center of your viewpoint.

### CHAPTER 5

# Why Charting a Course Is Important

Why is it necessary to chart a course? In our modern world, it isn't really necessary to make a detailed plan and map it out when traveling on land. We have personal satellite powered navigation at our fingertips almost all the time. We can get in the car and drive for days without ever needing a detailed plan, so long as we have a destination in mind, we can get there. If there is bad weather, we stop and carry on after it has passed. This ease and convenience changes dramatically when we add our travel plans into the constant and unpredictable environments of air and water.

The reason that a carefully laid plan is necessary for both air and water travel is that the environment in which you are traveling is constantly changing. It is continually shifting and affecting whether or not you will actually end up in the selected final destination. Elements like wind, currents, tide changes, storms, and even water depth will determine how quickly and directly we will end up at our selected destination. If you are not prepared to make adjustments when things change, you may end up in an entirely different place, or not arrive at all. Having a plan, being prepared, and persevering is the safest way to set out on a journey. Captains like Chelsea "Sully" Sullenburger (the pilot who safely landed US Airways flight 1549 on the Hudson River in 2009) don't become heroes because they hit the autopilot button; they spend years planning, adjusting, training, so that when tragedy is ahead they remain calm, and navigate their way to safe landings.[1]

How badly do you want to face adversity with calm, ease, and trust in the plan that God has for you?

**Jeremiah 29:11 / For I know the plans I have for you," declares the LORD, "plans to prosper you and not to harm you, plans to give you hope and a future. (NIV)**

If you need a huge dose of encouragement read through the scripture below, which always has given me courage.

**Psalm 91:1-16 (ESV)[2] /**
**[1]He who dwells in the shelter of the Most High will abide in the shadow of the Almighty.**
**[2]I will say to the LORD, "My refuge and my fortress, my God, in whom I trust!"**
**[3]For it is He who delivers you from the snare of the trapper and from the deadly pestilence.**
**[4]He will cover you with His pinions, And under His wings you may seek refuge; His faithfulness is a shield and bulwark.**
**[5]You will not be afraid of the terror by night, Or of the arrow that flies by day;**

<sup>6</sup>**Of the pestilence that stalks in darkness,**
   **Or of the destruction that lays waste at**
   **noon.**
<sup>7</sup>**A thousand may fall at your side**
   **And ten thousand at your right hand,**
   ***But* it shall not approach you.**
<sup>8</sup>**You will only look on with your eyes**
   **And see the recompense of the wicked.**
<sup>9</sup>**For you have made the LORD, my refuge,**
   ***Even* the Most High, your dwelling place.**
<sup>10</sup>**No evil will befall you,**
   **Nor will any plague come near your tent.**
<sup>11</sup>**For He will give His angels charge**
   **concerning you,**
   **To guard you in all your ways.**
<sup>12</sup>**They will bear you up in their hands,**
   **That you do not strike your foot against**
   **a stone.**
<sup>13</sup>**You will tread upon the lion and cobra,**
   **The young lion and the serpent you will**
   **trample down.**
<sup>14</sup>**"Because he has loved Me, therefore I will**
   **deliver him;**
   **I will set him *securely* on high, because**
   **he has known My name.**
<sup>15</sup>**"He will call upon Me, and I will answer**
   **him; I will be with him in trouble;**
   **I will rescue him and honor him.**
<sup>16</sup>**"With a long life I will satisfy him**
   **And let him see My salvation."**

It is no secret that life presents us with ever changing circumstances. We encounter a multitude of conditions and situations that are in constant flux. Things like our finances, our jobs, and our relationships are never truly stagnant. We move to new houses, we move to new cities, and we sometimes move to new countries. Personally, I don't want the sudden loss of a job or a loved one to throw my life so out of order that I forget who I am and what I was created to do.

Consider the image of a dad throwing his toddler high into the air. When the child first is launched skyward, their face is full of uncertainty. Once they descend and Dad catches them, they squeal with delight and typically beg to do it again. Similarly, when we make a decision to chart a course that is aligned to God's plan and purpose for our lives, we set ourselves up for the greatest adventure ever. Although we might get tossed by the sea, we learn to trust that God will be there to catch us in each and every moment.

Let's explore what it means to create a plan, to chart a course, that aligns with God's word and carefully begin the journey that leads to His purposes, His plans, and His safe harbors.

# Section 2

## Plan

### CHAPTER 6

# Determining Where We Are

As we prepare to develop a plan, we must determine where we are starting from. In regards to our sea navigation analogy, it can be as simple as pointing to the boat in the harbor. Other times it is as difficult as completing a challenging math equation using the sun, stars, and the estimated speed you have already traveled. This is also true in life. At times we are very aware of where we are starting from in relation to where we want to go, and other times we are completely in the dark.

For example, I have a great deal of feedback from where I am as a writer and teacher. I have a whole hard drive of started and unfinished stories, books, screenplays, poems, sermons, and songs. I know where I want to go and I know where I am starting from. This isn't always easy though, especially when it comes to emotional or spiritual health. Maybe we feel depressed, but we cannot put our finger on the exact reason "why." Or we just have no idea how to get out of our "funk."

Another example might be in our relationships with friends, a spouse, or a child where we don't know where we stand, but we would like to see a change. How do we determine our emotional or spiritual location in those cases? This is much like determining the location of a ship at sea, in the dark, while it is moving! It is tricky when the shoreline is long gone and we don't have much to grab a hold of. Especially when relationships go silent because of a situation or circumstance that was uncomfortable.

Have you ever had a situation where you were treated poorly by a friend or family member and rather than courageously addressing the hurt, you retreated into yourself? I read a story recently about a family who was dealing with the passing of their mother and the subsequent liquidation of the estate. The siblings fell into an all out war about how everything should be handled. Rather than looking to the word of God and the heart behind their mother's will they thought of their own needs over those of their entire family. This caused a major rift in the family for years! How do you walk back into healthy and loving relationships after you have been deeply hurt or abused?

The ancient sea navigators would look to the unchanging and consistent markers of the sun and the stars. It is no wonder that we must do the same thing. We must look to God's word and His creation for the unwavering markers to help us start from the right place. If we miscalculate where we are starting from, all the planning, preparation, and perseverance in the world will not get you to your intended destination.

Practically, what does this look like? You must set aside time to reflect on where you are and ask honestly for the truth. If you do not set aside enough quiet time, then the busyness of life will distract you from starting well. Quiet time spent alone seeking answers from God will never be a waste. When I really need guidance, I have to set aside ample time to get clarity. God is so faithful and He always shows up. When I need to understand where I am starting from and how far the journey might be, I ask myself the following set of questions:

- God, where I am starting from?
- With regards to my relationships?
- With regards to my goals or dreams?
- Show me a clear picture of my current situation and reveal to me those areas that I will need to be prepared for as I journey.

Write down any dreams, visions, thoughts and feedback that you receive.

Sometimes you will hear from God directly. Other times it will come from reading the Bible, or possibly by receiving feedback from trusted friends. I have had many friends confirm things I was called to do in my spirit. It can be painful when you ask God to reveal where you are. It can be convicting or fill you with a reluctance to even begin. Don't let this revelation deter you from pursuing His will, regardless of the difficulties you face. God is so loving that He will guide your every step in the journey. Keep in mind when you receive direction from God, He will never call you to lie, to steal, to harm another person, as it violates His law directly. However, he will stretch you beyond your current capacity.

- How is my attitude about where I am starting from?
- Is it healthy, or is it full of anxiety or fear?

When we are evaluating where we are starting, it is necessary for us to understand that our attitude will play a significant role in our progression. When we are facing a challenging situation it can cause us to be full of doubt, fear, and anxiety. That is natural! We just need to be aware of it before we set sail. Otherwise, those tricky emotions can sabotage us before we even pull up anchor.

I have many friends who struggle tremendously with anxiety and stress. Seemingly common events or situations can throw them into a panic. I don't want to passively dismiss this real feeling of being overwhelmed; however, the word of God calls us to capture negative thinking and make it obedient to Christ.

**2 Corinthians 10:5 / We break down every thought and proud thing that puts itself up against the wisdom of God. We take hold of every thought and make it obey Christ. (NLV)**[1]

Furthermore, it implores us to reflect on things that are positive. God created our thoughts to be powerful change agents that can manifest a reality. That is why he gave some guidelines on what to think about!

**Philippians 4:8 / "Finally, brothers, whatever is true, whatever is honorable, whatever is just, whatever is pure, whatever is lovely, whatever is commendable, if there is any excellence, if there is anything worthy of praise, think about these things." (NIV)**

An artist by the name of Francesca Reigler said, "Happiness is an attitude: we either make ourselves miserable, or happy and strong. The amount of work is the same."[2]

Perhaps you are thinking, "Yeah that all sounds great, but if you knew my history, you would know why I am so skeptical." Skepticism parades itself as wisdom to keep us stuck in a place of fear. I don't want to look back on my life with regret about a risk

I was unwilling to take because I lacked courage. "If you want to change your life, first you have to construct your new reality," touts Shawn Achor, author of *The Happiness Advantage*.[3]

Well-known psychologist Barbara Frederickson of the University of North Carolina has published a largely cited paper that demonstrates the reality that those who reflect more often on positive ideas, aspects, and outcomes actually experience and manifest more of those opportunities. This isn't science fiction, or just the power of positive thinking. God built our brains to CREATE, so having the right attitude will help us set the right course.[4]

Perform a quick check on your attitude:

- How do you feel about where you are at, and where you are headed?
- Does it cause fear and doubt, or excitement and wonder?

The same situation can produce either emotion. It depends on our choices and our willingness to capture the negative emotions and submit them to the authority of Christ. Our attitude is a choice; if you are particularly averse to risky living or moving into the unknown, ask for help in seeing the embarkation as an exciting adventure. Write down all of the potentially positive outcomes of the journey. Why do you feel God is calling you on this journey at this moment? I promise that taking a journey with Jesus at the helm of your ship will help you grow in grace, strength, and joy. Again, ask to be shown where you are currently positioned and how can you frame your journey in a positive light?

### Am I starting from a stable place or an unstable place?

As you are reading this you might actually be in crisis right now. You could be facing addictions, abuse, or soul-crushing depression.

Take heart, for the Lord is with you. He will teach you to navigate as you go, but you need to begin trusting in His direction today. Trust is the absence of fear. This might require you to reach out to others in faith that will help you. Don't allow fear to lock you in a prison; become the bondage breaker you have been praying to find. Whether or not you feel you are starting from a stable position, I encourage you to prayerfully consider your journey and take the time to hear clearly from God.

### CHAPTER 7

# Where are you going?

This is quite possibly the most challenging task when charting a course. It can be one of the most open-ended questions anyone ever asks you. Where do you want to go? What do you want to be? What are your biggest dreams? These are questions that can feel overwhelming. I know they are for me sometimes. I don't often give myself permission to ask these types of questions because I am afraid they will get in the way of what I feel pressured to do today. I am a wife, mother, business woman, volunteer, and writer. I don't have time to ponder what I want to do with my life. Life is already happening.

However, these types of questions trigger our brain to consider what is possible and explore the impossible. If we are going to properly chart our course we must ask God, dream with God, investigate our God-given gifts, and wait for His confirmation.

## *Ask God*

Start by asking God to reveal His plans to you. Set aside some prayer time to ask the following questions:

- Where do you want me to go?
- What do you want me to do?

First, approach God with a humble spirit as you ask. This requires a surrendering of our own personal desires and aspirations to follow God wherever He might lead us. It's freaky. It requires trust. We must believe that God will lead us AND that His plans are better than what we can devise on our own.

Second, we must tune into the still small voice of our Creator, and be patient enough to wait for the answer. You will face distractions, fear, doubt, and probably a sense of uncertainty as you begin to hear from God, but the great news is that He WANTS to show you His plans. He is not into confusion, or messages that require a diploma in ancient Greek. He will speak plainly and in a way that is comfortable for you. Just make sure you are taking time to clear your mind, calm your spirit, and quiet the noise in your life to actually hear.

God has spoken to me through many avenues: a trusted friend, His word, or a unique opportunity. However, I believe one of His favorite ways of speaking to all of us is through our dreams.

## *Permission to Dream*

Sugar Ray Leonard once said, "Dreams are life's GPS."[1] I love this quote because it gives us a clear analogy of how our dreams, our desires, and goals help us to find turn-by-turn directions. What are your heart's desires? What are your dreams? What do you want to be when you grow up? What's on the bucket list? Begin to visualize yourself on the journey, and start to get clues as to where God is leading.

**Psalm 37:4 / Delight yourself in the Lord, and He will give you the desires of your heart. (ESV)**

When is the last time you asked yourself, "What are my dreams?" That question caused me to panic and feel discouraged at one point in my journey.

Alex and I were out to dinner when Kennedy and Truman were four and three, respectively. I had spent the past four years just keeping the house from falling apart and hadn't given much thought to what I wanted out of life. He caught me off-guard when he asked me, "What are your dreams?"

I almost burst into tears because I hadn't asked myself that question since I had gotten married. I immediately felt a flood of emotions including fear, hopelessness, and excitement all at once. It was almost as if I didn't have any dreams at all. I had diminished my dreams into survival, to just keep the plates spinning. It was depressing.

I scrambled to answer: "I don't know; raise great kids and continue to love you."

WAIT WHAT! That cannot be all. Can it? Not that those are not great goals, but I felt like I had a lot more in me. Maybe I was just delusional? Don't we all think we are destined to be something? Make an impact? Be a global world changer? I didn't feel like I had the capacity to become any of those; I felt like a loser.

Alex didn't buy the canned answer, and continued to press me on what MY dreams were. He wasn't asking about what I was already doing, but what were those destinations outside of my comfort zone, and outside of my current abilities. It was crushing. In a panic I fell back on old dreams, those ghosts of my past to become an actress. It was a laughable response, and not properly explored. As I was sitting across from my husband, I felt like a failure, I felt like a fake, and I felt like I had given up my own dreams to support those of my family. Alex encouraged me to think about what I wanted to do in life. He breathed new life into my sails.

The funny thing about giving ourselves permission to dream about our future is that God is already waiting there for us. He knows what we are capable of, and He has equipped each of us to change our world. Literally, every single one of us is a world changer, if you can believe that. It's amazing! Not everyone will have a legacy like that of Martin Luther King, Jr., or Bill Gates, or Mother Teresa, but each of us is will make changes in the world around us.

**Ephesians 2:10 / For we are God's masterpiece. He has created us anew in Christ Jesus, so we can do the good things he planned for us long ago. (NLT)**[2]

That conversation with Alex sparked something inside me. I was ready to see where God wanted me to go next.

### *God: your dream partner*

Inviting God to inform your dreams gives you liberty to explore uncharted waters. After all, you are not journeying alone. You are planning a trip with the most well-resourced, knowledgeable captain in the universe. Just because YOU don't have all the pieces of the dream sorted doesn't mean they are not from God. "If your dreams don't scare you, they are not big enough," said Ellen Johnson Sirleaf.[3] I would say, if your dreams don't scare you, they didn't come from God.

God wants to partner with us in accomplishing our dreams.

If we can do it all in our own strength, with our own resources, and with our own ideas, then we don't need God. Some of us who are lovingly called "control freaks" have a harder time envisioning things outside of what seems realistic. If this is you, preface your dream statements with the possibility that time and money are unlimited. For example,

*If money and time were limitless, I would . . .*

If God calls you to it, He will resource you through it.

Maybe you never thought of yourself as an entrepreneur, but you had this idea you think would make a great business. Explore that more! See what kinds of relationships, opportunities, and events you might find yourself attending or hosting. Perhaps you have a dream of opening a school, but you are not an educator. Explore what your school offers: who are the instructors, and what kinds of certifications would be required? God's specialty is the miraculous, inconceivable, and "out of this world." He wants a partnership, so let's make sure to leave some space for His supernatural plan to unfold.

### Unique gifts and talents

As we begin to explore our dreams, we want to pay close attention to the unique God-given talents and abilities He has built into us. Our interests and hobbies can tell us a lot about where God wants to send us. You might have a particular interest in floral arranging, or music, or even an odd love for spreadsheets (God bless you if you love spreadsheets!). Perhaps you have a special, patient heart with people that have dementia or young children. Look to where you find yourself naturally attracted. Look for open doors in those areas and listen carefully to what God may say.

One of the gifts God has blessed me with is having the ability to tell a good story. I started out by telling other people's stories, but once I surrendered my life to Jesus, I started sensing the nudge to write stories of my own. Our unique gifts and talents will produce spiritual fruit when they are put to use. For me as a writer, when I have been faithful in completing short stories, monologues, and poems they brought peace and love and joy to the lives of those that heard or read them.

I remember an instance where I woke up in the middle of the night and God put a good friend of mine on my heart. He gave me the words "stained glass heart." My friend was going through an absolutely horrific divorce where her husband had committed adultery with a much younger woman and had destroyed his family. My friend was a faith-filled woman struggling with her trust in God and the current state of her heart.

Unbeknownst to me, she had been praying for weeks for God to show her what her heart looked like. I wrote a poem that described what had happened to her heart and how God was planning on putting all the pieces back together into a beautiful stained glass heart that would reflect His light and holiness. It was a deeply personal piece of writing and I was so nervous when I sent it to her. I didn't hear back right away and felt that maybe I had missed the mark. Did I not hear God right? Did I somehow offend her? What if I added to her hurt? Much later, my friend confessed to me that my poem had saved her from suicide a number of times. She would read it over and over again as an encouragement to her soul.

As you explore your gifts and talents, look for where you are making an impact. Where are you bringing peace, joy, patience, goodness, and kindness into the world? These are markers for God at work in you and through you. They will help to clarify where He is leading!

## *Wait for Confirmation*

For me and, I am sure, for many others, the waiting is the most difficult part of determining where God is prompting you to go. I have often found myself in a period where I felt like I was in limbo, waiting for the next direction. I may have an inkling of where I am headed, but waiting on confirmation isn't easy. Patience has never been a virtue that came easily to me, so my journey is often-times full of opportunities to develop patience. Many times I have received a vision or a direction from God and then a whole season or chapter of life passes before anything manifests into reality.

I remember a time when God laid a burden on my heart for the men of His house. I noticed a distinct difference between the men I saw in church every week and Alex. They were men that had been suppressed and were prohibited to be silly, get dirty, yell, grunt, and yes, fart! A true godly man is not a soft-handed, passive, emotional wreck. He is a force to be reckoned with. He is full of love and compassion that has a distinctly masculine signature. He is not without fault, but he thrives under the challenges of the Ultimate Coach. Alex represented this ideal in my mind and I wanted all of my friends' husbands to be inspired to believe for the same kind of expression.

I felt led to write a monologue, a kind of epic battle cry for Christian men. It was written in the style of *Braveheart* or *Gladiator*, but the topic was about the men of God's house taking up arms. A manifesto encouraging them to no longer be content with the abuse, perversion, and bullying that exists in the world.

At any rate, along with the monologue, I had a secondary thought of building a weekend retreat where men were allowed and encouraged to do manly stuff. My expectation was that this retreat and the speech would end up launching into some form of men's ministry in the very near future.

The truth is, the vision went stone cold silent for five years. I wrote the speech and passed around the retreat idea with some level of modest interest but it went into hibernation. I didn't really even think about it again until we moved back from the UK and settled in Phoenix.

One night we went out on a massive couples outing and I posed the question to all the men at the table, "What kind of activities would you want to do on a boys weekend?" That question was like electricity shooting through the atmosphere. As soon as they all started dreaming and collaborating, you could feel the excitement rise.. It was as if the inner boy was screaming, "Yeah, when do we get to do this?" The following week my campus pastor asked me for the list I had jotted down during the evening in order to begin an activity-based men's ministry!

The point is, the timing from when you receive an inkling in your spirit to when that comes to fruition can vary.

A word of caution: while you wait, don't settle for inactivity. It takes a lot more effort to push a stationary ship than to steer a moving one.

What do you do while you wait? My recommendation is to pray, read the word, and remind yourself of all the things God has already done in your life. Those activities will draw you back to God's truth and reinforce trust in His timing.

I am ALWAYS on the move, so my personal struggle is slowing down and trusting in God's speed for my life. For example, if you are driving 70 mph down a street that has a 35 mph speed limit, you are probably going to miss the turn God has earmarked up ahead. You will likely blow right past that turn and many others unless you slow down and take the right pace to make sure you don't keep going in circles. Practice the art of being patient as you continue to let God work, while you wait to see the dream placed in your heart come to fruition.

### CHAPTER 8

# Setting Your Course Bearing

In terms of navigation,t setting a bearing is all about the direction in which the ship is moving in relation to true north. This is expressed in degrees and is something that will change constantly as circumstances shift. Even if there is a direct path to your final destination, that bearing will vary with wind, water depth, currents, and the changing of tides.

Once you have spent time listening for God and feel you have received confirmation on where you are going, it is time to ask for the next step. Setting a course bearing in terms of our spiritual journey is about a process of asking, and waiting for the sequence of turn-by-turn directions.

Rarely do we get a fully fleshed out plan with all the details on how to make it to the end goal or vision. Usually God just shows us the next step or two in the journey. He only gives us as much as we need, and as much as we can handle.

I read this analogy on a blog by Catrina Welch that equates God's directions to the guidance we get from a GPS.[1] The tool doesn't give us every turn for the entire trip and then expect us to remember. It waits until we are nearly to the next turn and then lets us know which way to go. God works similarly whereby He will nudge us to adjust our bearing just before it needs to happen. If we miss the turn, the beauty is that God will "recalculate" just like our GPS!

God's turn-by-turn guidance can sometimes be as simple as picking up the phone and making a call to a friend you haven't spoken to in years. Other times it might mean taking a significant faith step, like asking someone to marry you.

If I had known all of the turns and the kind of difficulties we would face when we moved to the UK, I would never have made the choice to go.

Alex and I spent our five year wedding anniversary in London and his boss, at the time, asked him to go on a business meeting (I know, right . . .anniversary and business meeting do not mix, but more on that another time). After Alex had gone on this meeting, his boss asked if we would be interested in moving to the UK. This was the first nudge that there was the possibility of a major change coming.

Alex and I had talked years before about living abroad and thought it would be a great adventure, but never really entertained the thought further. We laughed at the opportunity and had to pinch ourselves several times thinking it couldn't be real. We began praying about what this meant, and God continued to open doors. It was a systematic progression that certainly wasn't without distractions. There were so many reasons for us not to go, and very few logical motives to take this leap of faith. We had just bought a home in Connecticut. We had two babies aged three and two. We had my in-laws only three hours away when we needed help with the kids. We liked our community and Alex was making a good living. We were content. However, we felt that nudge over and over again that God was leading us overseas to a new adventure. We started the journey of exploring the option, which meant we were already headed out to sea. Our GPS was set and we were getting moment-by-moment instructions leading to our European adventure.

One of the directions we were given was that we were being called to a new church in England. Before we moved we traveled back to London to find a suitable home and neighborhood. While we were house-hunting we explored possible church homes as well. On Sunday morning we prayed for a divine appointment with a family that had children and could tell us about the culture of the church we were planning to visit.

Word to the wise, be specific in how you pray for confirmation that you are going in the right direction!

God didn't fail us.

When we got to the church we met a lovely woman who had a son a few months older than my son. Alex and I spent the afternoon at lunch with this family. The crazy part was that they happened to be the Pastor and his wife and son! The encouraging words they expressed about the plans and direction of the church were directly in line with our hearts desires. After this experience, Alex and I knew we were moving to England. It was then that we firmly set the bearing of our ship toward Europe. It was exciting, but once we had done this, we came against all kinds of headwinds and hurdles to overcome in order to move.

We went into ridiculous negotiations with the company. We

had to sell everything we owned. We had to put our house on the market. It seemed impossible, but we walked in faith as God led us around each bend. We went through a series of shallow reefs having to slow down and manage all the tiny details to get to open water. From the time that we went on our anniversary trip to when we moved into our new house in Weybridge, UK, it was six months almost to the day. It felt lightening fast.

I remember two weeks before we left the US I was crying at my mother-in-law's house that I didn't want to go. "Why do we have to go?" I asked. It was my flesh raging against the will of God. I had thrown out my anchor even though we were already far from the known shoreline. It didn't feel like my bearing was pointed toward True North; I was unsure we were following our Heavenly Father. It was like I was heading into limbo, the unknown. I was voyaging without any safety net whatsoever. I had spent so much time looking down at those little reefs, trying to avoid collision, that I didn't realize how close I was to opening up the sails and moving fast. Fear was trying to hold me back and confuse me. My bearing was set precisely according to God's will.

When your bearing is right, you will experience great spiritual growth. That is not to say that everything will be smooth sailing. The main safety net for setting the right bearing is focusing your attention and your heart on Jesus. That might seem ethereal and not very practical. I would be asking the same question: "Yes, but HOW do I do that?" It boils down to making a simple request over and over again, "God, show me the way." Then surrendering to His leading. The more often you ask, the more likely you will get a response and you will begin to "ride the waves" and not get tossed around by them.

### CHAPTER 9

# Consulting the Compass Rose

Have you ever felt like you were out in the middle of the ocean, with no clue which way to go next? I know I have taken steps to follow God's lead and then questioned whether or not I took a wrong turn because I stopped seeing the visible markers that determined my course bearing was accurate. In those moments I find myself saying, "God, where are you? Did I miss something? Hello? HELLO!" These are instances when we must leverage our tools and employ new techniques to tune into the guidance of the Holy Spirit.

Please bear with me as I try to simplify a few technical sailing strategies.

As previously mentioned, the compass rose is an important tool that indicates the variance between magnetic north and true north.[1] It was particularly useful for sailors when they needed to make accurate modifications. It was critically necessary when they could no longer see recognizable landmarks. The use of the compass rose was employed specifically when practicing certain techniques, such as dead reckoning, a technique used to determine current positions based on a previously determined location, and taking into account known speeds and time passed.[2]

As you can imagine, dead reckoning methods were fraught with errors and could set back a ship's arrival by a significant amount. For example, consider Christopher Columbus' journey across the Atlantic. If he had traveled straight across, he would have discovered New Jersey, but instead he ended up in the Bahamas. Perhaps this was a divine detour. After all, who wouldn't want to end up in the Bahamas after traveling for months at sea? All this to say that even the most advanced and skilled sailors make mistakes and are required to modify their plans in order to arrive safely.

This is relevant to our journey with God as our True North, the never changing point that we always have to point us in the right direction. The Holy Spirit acts as our compass rose, indicating whether or not we are traveling toward or away from God's purpose and plans for our life.

The Holy Spirit will help us remain sensitive to God amidst the ever-changing circumstances of life, and fill us with the power to persevere and overcome obstacles. When we learn to fine tune our ears to hear the whisperings of the Holy Spirit, we are positioned well, even when we no longer have any landmarks signifying that we are on track. When we are feeling like we are out in the middle of nowhere, we should consult the Holy Spirit to confirm our course heading. Our spiritual dead reckoning precision lies squarely on how responsive we are to the guidance of the Holy Spirit.

### *How do we hear from the Holy Spirit?*

Some people hear the audible voice of the Holy Spirit, like a unique voice inside their head. Others may sense a nudge or leading in their heart. Still others experience the guidance of the Holy Spirit through intense study of the Bible, through community in church, and changes in circumstances. In my journey I have had all of these experiences, at one point or another.

One of the most significant audible experiences happened shortly after I met Alex. We met at a personal training certification conference that was held in California, just north of Los Angeles. I sat right next to Alex and introduced myself, even though the whole room was open. I figured I would try to make a friend as I had recently moved to California from New York.

He looked like a typical jock, with long, curly surfer hair and arms that resembled tree trunks. He was very friendly and accommodated me with my barrage of questions. It was easy to find things to talk about, and Alex asked if I wanted to carpool for the rest of the conference. I immediately said yes because I was basically broke and saving ten dollars was amazing at the time.

On the final day of the conference we were riding back to Los Angeles and a Christian song began to play in Alex's car. He let it play for a moment and then went to change it, but I stopped him, saying I liked the song. He asked if I was a Christian and where I went to church. I explained that I was a Christian but I was still searching for a church home.

He invited me to his church the following weekend, and I agreed, saying I would love to check it out. Alex then said, "Hey, we should celebrate finishing the certification, let's go out for dinner." I said, "Sure."

The date was awful. I mean terrible, awful, and one of the worst, most boring dates I can remember. I felt like I was on a date with my brother; we could talk for days but there was no chemistry. None. I later found out Alex felt the same way. Regardless of our lack of romantic interest, we both agreed to stay in touch and planned to go to church together the following Sunday.

I had a personal training client cancel on Saturday and ask if they could reschedule for Sunday morning. Again, I was broke so I had to change my plans to visit Alex's church. I called him and apologized for having to reschedule and told him I would make it up to him by making him dinner. I explained that the church I was attending had an evening service. If he wanted to join me afterward, I would cook.

All Alex needed to hear was the word cook. He was a bachelor living on grilled chicken and frozen vegetables, so anything homemade was likely going to be better.

We went to the evening service and this is where the Holy Spirit knocked me for a loop.

The pastor asked us to pray for one another during an extended time of prayer and worship. Alex began calling out insecurities that were as though he was reading the pain written on my heart. He spoke words of healing and restoration over me. Then I cried. Like the ugly, sniffling, snot-dripping kind of crying. It was not pretty. I couldn't control it, though. All the damage I had done to myself and allowed other men to do to me started to unravel. After Alex finished praying we went back to a moment of worship and this is when I heard the voice.

It said, "Let go of your past hurt, and give in to the love this man has for you."

WHAT! I thought I must be having a nervous breakdown. I was hearing voices, and it was telling me to give in to the love of a guy I only met seven days ago. Plus, I already knew I wasn't attracted to this guy; remember the awful date? Regardless, I sensed that this voice somehow was leading me to wholeness.

I said to myself, "What do I have to lose?" I resigned myself to see where it would go.

Alex and I left that service with fresh eyes. It was as though the service was the lens cleaner. The Holy Spirit whispered to both our hearts and dusted off our glasses. We saw each other as the creation God designed us to be, and boy, was that different! Alex suddenly became this incredibly sensitive, handsome, and gentle man of faith. A man full of power and self-confidence without any of the arrogance. Needless to say, I was wildly attracted to him!

From that moment on Alex and I began to date officially. We were married 18 months later.

I was so grateful I was sensitive to the voice of the Holy Spirit that night. Even though I felt like I was out in the middle of the ocean with no indication that this would work out, I didn't let my previous experience with the bad date deter me from following the guidance of the Holy Spirit. It ultimately led to one of the best gifts God has blessed me with.

If you have never felt the presence of the Holy Spirit, or you are unsure if you have heard the audible voice of God, ask Him to show you how to find Him. I know you might be thinking, it cannot be that easy. Ask the all powerful, omniscient Creator of the universe and He will talk to me? Invite the Holy Spirit to begin leading and guiding you.

He will.

God desires a relationship with us more than anything, and he sent His Son to prove it. In the secular world you will often hear the phrase "follow your heart," which, if tuned properly to the Holy Spirit, will lead to God's will and plan for your life.

Whether it is an audible voice, intense study of the Bible,

changes in circumstances, or an impression in your spirit, pay close attention to what the Holy Spirit might be nudging you toward. The Holy Spirit, like the compass rose, helps us to stay on course. He reveals the adjustments we need to make to align ourselves with the plans God has.

As you get more adept at being sensitive to the Holy Spirit, a whole new world will begin to unfold for you. You will see people as you never have before and you will go places that you never thought possible.

# Section 3

## Prepare

### CHAPTER 10

# Prepare vs. Plan

I was worried the "plan" and "prepare" sections were going to sound too similar, but the more I reflected on it, the more I discovered that they are in fact distinctly different. When you begin the process of setting out on a journey, you not only create a plan on how to get there, but you also prepare for that journey. I equate the plan to the drawing of the projected course lines on the map. Imagine an old movie where you travel the map by connected lines that are either animated by a plane, train, bus, or boat; that's the plan! Even in our modern day we plan a trip by booking our tickets, hotels, rental cars, etc. We build an itinerary. Then we prepare for it by packing all that we might need and possibly even learning new things about the culture or place we are planning to visit.

Let your mind think about the preparation that was required for a sea voyage back in the early 1300s. Stockpiling enough food in case you drifted far off course and didn't arrive at the destination at the expected time. Equipping the ship with the necessary equipment to survive should you start taking on water. Training sailors in the art of naval warfare if pirates were encountered. Ensuring your crew was properly trained to respond to the inevitable changes that occur at sea. Even today modern sailors don't dare to attempt a long voyage without first successfully navigating several hundred local trips.

The most important things in preparing for a long voyage would be to gather resources and provisions, including gaining insight. Second would be to train properly to prevent catastrophic loss, and avoid as many hazards as possible. Lastly, and this could be the most important, is to ask yourself if you are courageous enough to embark on this adventure. Even if you don't necessarily feel like setting sail, you need enough audacity and faith to trust God's plan and provision. As my Pastor Brian Houston says, "Get that pioneering spirit."

### CHAPTER 11

# Resources — Provision, Time, and Expertise

I have been discouraged when I felt called to do something or to step out in faith, but the resources I currently had were not enough. Whether it was a lack in the bank account or a lack of time, I hesitated to even begin. I am prone to limit myself, and my goals, because I don't have what I think I need in hand.

Have you put a God-sized dream in a box because you couldn't figure out how to resource it? Or perhaps you felt you didn't have the right expertise or education to bring the dream into reality. I think these gaps are purposeful in growing our faith in God's ability to provide. In order for us to set out on our journey with God we must overcome our fear of lack.

## Psalm 23:1 / The Lord is my shepherd, I shall not want.

I shall not want means I will lack nothing. I will have all that I need to accomplish what I am called to do. There are three areas that I think are relevant to our journey: resources, time, and expertise.

### *Resources*

No matter where God is calling you, you will need resources. You might need finances or a building space, you might need to travel or a vehicle or equipment. The specific needs will be determined by where you are trying to go. Just like you would create a packing list before you go on a trip, you will want to make a list of resources you feel are necessary. Pray for God to reveal what you should add to your list. Once you have compiled the resources you require, check off those items you already have or have access to, and which items you need to believe God for. If you are truly following God's plan, there will be a few items on this list that are out of reach.

- Compile a list of needs
- Check off the resources you already have or have access to
- Highlight specific resources you believe God will provide

I want to share a part of the story found in Exodus 14-17 to encourage you to believe for miraculous resources.

The nation of Israel was set free from slavery in Egypt with enough resources to get to the promised land. It was an eleven day journey that ended up taking 40 years. There was no way they would have been able to stockpile enough provisions for a journey that long. Once the food and water were gone, the Israelites began to grumble.

This lack of faith and ungrateful attitude caused God to want to wipe out the entire nation. Fortunately, Moses trusted in God's plan. He knew God was leading the voyage and He would arrange a way for all that was needed. God didn't fail to provide because of Moses' faith. God rained down food from the sky in the form of manna. An entire nation of people were fed daily by collecting just what they needed. If they collected more manna than they needed it would rot before the next day. God trained them to rely on His provision each and every day.

God gives us just enough to live on, to save and invest overtime, trusting in His process and small incremental growth. It is a daily decision to believe God will provide for our needs.

When Jesus taught us to pray in the famous prayer "Our Father," he said, "Give us this day our DAILY bread." He didn't say give us all that we will need to accomplish Your plan for our lives.

A personal example of how God provided miraculously for my needs happened when we moved to Phoenix. We could only afford to ship our clothes and some sentimental items as we left the UK. We had to sell or donate all of our furniture, because it was more expensive to have it shipped across the Atlantic than to purchase new when we arrived. The one caveat was that we barely had enough money to ship our personal items back home, much less purchase new furniture.

Once we were able to get settled into our own house (albeit a rental), we created a list of the resources we needed. Then we made a plan to purchase items one month at a time. The first month we planned to buy beds, the second month the dining table and chairs, the third month the sofa, and so on. We were humbly trusting that eventually we would have what we needed for our home.

When we were doing a walk through of the home that we ended up renting, the woman who lived there told us she was downsizing. She was leaving a big corporate job and launching her own business. She was a single mother of a young daughter, so they were moving into an apartment and were selling most of the furniture in the house. As we walked through she said, "Please let me know if you want anything, otherwise I am having a clearing company come and bulk purchase the rest."

This woman had spent the better part of 20 years in retail and had the most impeccable taste. Her home was beautiful, and I loved EVERYTHING! Alex and I sat down and compared our list to what was available in the home. We laughed because it was almost everything. Who were we kidding? We didn't have anything! We sent the woman an offer for the amount we were planning on spending to buy our beds the first month. We explained to her that while we loved everything, this was all we were able to offer. Alex told her to please let us know what she would be willing to part with for that amount.

She responded saying she accepted the lump sum offer for every piece of furniture in the house, including two beds for our kids! I literally wept out loud in front of Costco. People must have thought I was a lunatic but I didn't care. I was crying and saying, "God is so good, God is so good, thank you, Jesus, thank you, thank you."

God knew our needs and He made a way where there wasn't any way visible. If you are struggling with a need for resources, pray that God will increase your faith. Faith precedes provision. We believe and then we receive.

## *Time*

Maybe what you lack is more of an intangible resource like "time." Have you ever heard of the phrase you need to make time? Well I'm sure you are already well aware that is impossible for you, but not for God! He created time, and He actually made time stop for one of his faith-filled children. Read the story of Joshua for full details.

**Joshua 10:12-13 / On the day the Lord gave the Amorites over to Israel, Joshua said to the Lord in the presence of Israel: "Sun, stand still over Gibeon, and you, moon, over the Valley of Aijalon." So the sun stood still, and the moon stopped, till the nation avenged itself on its enemies, as it is written in the Book of Jashar. The sun stopped in the middle of the sky and delayed going down about a full day. (NIV)**

In this story Joshua is battling fiercely against an enemy and needs more time to ensure victory. He knew that if the sun set and the enemy had time to rest and regroup, the battle would last too long for his troops to win. He pleads with God to make the sun stop in the sky. God stopped time to ensure His chosen people were victorious.

Have you ever had a late night out, followed by a big event the next day? Have you ever thought about praying for a multiplication of sleep?

I do this often. I need an average of seven to eight hours of sleep, so when I dip into the six hour or less a night, I am not very pleasant the next day. I pray that God will make my six hours feel like eight. I pray this over my children when they have to stay up late to finish homework, or we go out to eat as a family on a weeknight and get home past their normal bedtime.

I also have prayed for a spirit of alertness well into the evening when I have had to work late. My brain is most effective between the hours of 10am to 1pm, so when I have had to push my writing time into the evening, the results have been less than great. When I cannot write in the morning, I ask God to help me stay alert during the time I am able to commit.

If you feel pressed for time already but you realize your journey will require extra time, look for areas of your life that can either be eliminated or changed. Be aggressive in cutting out tasks that are not a priority, and ask God to help you find time.

Some ways God can help you make time:

- Help you eliminate distractions and unnecessary things from your schedule
- Multiply sleep
- Help you to be more efficient and focused

Just because we have God on our side doesn't mean we are reckless with our time. We must protect our time more than any other resource because it is limited by 24 hours in each day. We don't get those hours back once they are gone. We must be strategic and ask God how to use our time. Only after we have done what we can in the natural, then we pray for God to bring supernatural time extensions.

### *Expertise*

The last thing you might feel you lack as you begin following God is a lack of expertise or insight. Let me encourage you: no one starts with the credibility they desire; expertise is gained over time. Furthermore, you personally don't have to possess all the necessary expertise to pull off the entire journey. A crew on a ship has a captain, first mate, deck hands, chef, and a myriad of other roles. It takes many different people and specialties to successfully navigate a ship to the final destination. Seek out mentors and people that are willing to consult with you to help you gain insight and wisdom.

One thing is for certain: if God is calling you to something, He already has the resources in mind that you will need and He is ready to manifest them in His perfect timing. Sometimes a lack of trust for the "stuff" we need will prevent us from moving forward with our journey. Don't let that be you. If you lack faith, ask God to help you with your disbelief.

**Mark 9:24 / Immediately the boy's father exclaimed, "I do believe; help me overcome my unbelief!" (NIV)**

# Training and Hazard Prevention

Even if you are not planning on becoming an expert, continuing to educate ourselves is a part of the journey. Many careers require some level of continuing education in order to stay relevant. Our spiritual journey is no different, and it will require a commitment to continue to learn. We will learn more about God's ways, learn more about being humble, learn more about listening instead of talking all the time. My list of "learnings" continues to grow almost daily.

**Proverbs 18:15 / An intelligent heart acquires knowledge, and the ear of the wise seeks knowledge. (ESV)**

Part of the preparation for a long sea voyage is to understand known hazards and the standard methods of avoiding or dealing with them. Seasoned sailors were well versed on how to handle the weather, as well as geographical and equipment-related hazards.

An example of this hazard prevention training has begun to reveal itself as I learn how to be a better parent. God has begun the process of teaching me about teenage disaster recovery. When I had my daughter I was so confident I would love her just the way that she needed to be loved. That I would never hurt or offend her.

I carried around a lot of confusion about my identity and my relationships with both my mom and dad until I was in my early twenties. I knew I was loved if I was perfect and excelled in everything I attempted. The lie I believed was, "If you fail, you will fall out of our good graces." I tested failure when I went away to college, just as many young people do once they are out on their own. I wanted to see what would happen if I didn't "follow the rules." I found that nothing happened to my relationship with my parents; however, I recognized that my choices to "fail" only destroyed my own self worth. My rebellion took the form of foul language, drinking, and probably the worst of them all, the promiscuity. I lowered my self respect to experience more and fit in with others who had already had far more intimate tragedies than I did.

I wanted to help my daughter avoid as much of this as I could. I doted on her, told her I love her and I am proud of her a lot! You can imagine my shock when I had to reprimand her and she broke down crying, in hysterics, and said, "I don't feel like you love me, Mommy." My whole world felt like it was breaking into a million pieces. How could she not know how much I love her? I correct her because I want her to be better than I am, and to be saved from all the heartache and confusion I experienced. I knew, however, that this was God's way of highlighting that the same lie had gotten into my own daughter's heart. This was a moment where I had to learn preventative measures and counter tactics to overcome this potential tsunami of doubt and fear.

I have stacks of books on parenting a "tween or teen" biblically. This is an area where I have a time deficit for sure, but I try and stash one of these books in my car, my purse, and on my night-stand so that as I gain fifteen minutes here and there, I can read them. In addition to my goodwill to read more about the topic, I am also asking parents who have children a bit older than mine if they ever dealt with similar issues and how. I pray that I will be able to train and equip her for God's plan for her life and, most impor-tantly, get her to know and trust that she is loved beyond measure. Loved by God and by me and by her Dad.

This little snafu in my grand plan has caused me to seek out some additional training as a parent and to pay closer attention to the warning signs my daughter is exhibiting. This experience was like a ripple in the water surface, signifying that a shallow reef may lie ahead. It was telling me, "Don't keep going straight!" I needed to find new ways to reinforce her internal confidence in God's love and replace the "I'm not loved" lie with the truth that she is loved beyond her behavior.

What warning signs are you or those around you exhibiting? Are there any hazards or possible hurdles you might need to over-come? Ask God to make you aware of those potential hazards as you journey. Anytime we are called to move outside of our com-fort zone there is a potential for danger, but when we stay focused on God's word and His ways, we can safely pass through restless waters.

Where can I find training for my journey?
Are there any additional books I can read?
Is there a mentor I can find?

In addition to answering the questions above, it might be useful to make a list of all the possible terrors you might encounter. Then take a giant red pen and write "JESUS" over them. In life we will encounter trials, distractions, chaos, and possible tragedy, but we have victory in Christ Jesus. We can do all things through Him. Surrender all the horrible "what if's" to Jesus.

We will never move forward with a positive attitude and a pioneering spirit if we allow our preparation to scare us away from taking the journey.

### CHAPTER 13

# Setting Sail

Now that you have written down all the possibly horrible things that could happen, say goodbye to safety! The next part of the journey is actually pulling up anchor and setting sail. This is an act of sheer faith. At times it is exciting because you are thrilled to be moving away from your current scenario; other times it will be incredibly nerve-wracking.

Imagine for a moment the sailors of old leaving the comforts of home, family, and safe harbor to sail across the sea. Maybe it was to discover new lands, which was an exciting time full of hope and potential. However, how about those that are just on the ship to gain a paycheck and recognize that they might never return? How would either perspective change the way in which adversity was dealt with? A man full of hope for a future will stare a storm in the face and use ALL the resources available both physically, mentally, and spiritually in order to succeed. Whereas a "hired hand" will quickly jump ship when rough waters occur.

**John 10: 12-13 / The hired hand is not the shepherd and does not own the sheep. So when he sees the wolf coming, he abandons the sheep and runs away. Then the wolf attacks the flock and scatters it. The man runs away because he is a hired hand and cares nothing for the sheep. (NIV)**

Are you in charge of making decisions on the journey or are you just along for the ride? The level of ownership you choose to take on your journey will make a significant difference in your experience.

One thing can be certain: changes will occur and your existing sense of safety or comfort will be challenged. Whatever you have grown accustomed to, whether it be a good or bad situation, is about to change, and that is unsettling for most people. Some individuals are so paralyzed by the fear of change that they never leave the comfort of their existing situation.

I have always been one to embrace new adventures, but I grow tired quickly. As boredom sets in, the temptation to moan and whine is strong. My maturity as an obedient and joy-filled Christian wanes as my inner child says, "Are we there yet?"

Specifically, times where I have been in a season of limbo have been particularly difficult. For example, for some time I have felt lead to join the ministry and have had several experiences where God gave me a vision of my future, and friends and acquaintances spoke prophetic words affirming this over me. But then I waited.

At first, when these visions and inklings began, I thought, "Nah, that's really not for me." However, over time, I realized how much I loved seeing people released from their prisons of shame, guilt, and doubt. I would share one word from God's truth that would alleviate their pain, or another that encouraged them to pursue something they never thought possible. It was so exhilarating. God began to show me allegories and illustrations about who He was in my life. It was exciting and I was ready to jump into the church and serve my guts out. But again I waited.

As I sailed toward this vision, God sent me to a group of individuals I would never have chosen on my own. I was called to work in sales with university professors. Let me tell you, they are a challenging group, certainly when it comes to faith. God specifically called me to instructors of math and science who have a particularly difficult time with faith in an unseen, immeasurable, and intangible God.

You can imagine my shock and disappointment when I began interviews and they went really well. I went through seven rounds of interviews for this role and all along the way I was praying against it. I didn't want to work in this industry; I wanted to work for church. However, God revealed to me one day He was calling me to the atheists and agnostics so that in their time of need, someone who knew Him would be there to pray and bless them.

WOW! I was totally convicted and I surrendered my will and said, "Okay, Lord, send me." I turned my course heading toward serving this particular group of people and boy, did I pick a fight. It was a consistent uphill battle trying to please, serve, and help this group of extremely intelligent and yet oftentimes arrogant group of people.

Many of them were very polite and kind, so I don't want to roll them all into a stereotype. However there were others that were rude, condescending, impatient, and blamed me personally when things in their courses went wrong. I had to swallow my pride everyday. There was even an incident where a professor blatantly flirted with me knowing full well I am happily married. I felt like I was in the trenches daily and loathed going to work. Again, I was moaning about the journey. I had to go to battle against my own mind and ask for a perspective change. Always keeping in mind that I am serving Jesus by serving them.

Here is the interesting thing: I am not a doormat type person, so my flesh rages strongly against rude behavior. I had to surrender my own desire to correct this rudeness and teach basic manners. I had to get better at stating the facts, apologizing for things that were out of my control, and continue to visit the very people that treated me like dirt. It was not easy.

The safety of my church family and people who already knew Christ was where I longed to be, but that was not where God was sending me. One day I read a devotional by Oswald Chambers that stated, "If you serve humanity only, they will wear you out. But if you serve Jesus Christ, you will be continually renewed even when people treat you like a doormat."[1] BOOM! Jesus was speaking directly to me about my heart toward my job and the customers I was serving. I didn't have a good attitude and it was jeopardizing my ability to show them the truth of the gospel.

Practically speaking, I had to quit longing for the future and start living in the present. The present was preparing me for the future, if I would let it.

I had pulled up the anchor already, but I needed to trust that God was going to bring me to where He had called me to be.

Setting sail is a bold and brave choice to surrender yourself to the uncertain, the unknown, and possibly, the uncomfortable.

Don't be too discouraged, though, because no matter what your present circumstances are, they won't be your long term reality. Every part of your journey is a season. If you are in a really peaceful, pleasant season, enjoy it! If you are not, pray for the endurance and perspective to go through it with peace and joy in your heart. Peer through God's looking glass to see what beautiful islands lie ahead. It serves as a reminder when fear and doubt tell you to stay home.

# Section 4

# Persevere

### CHAPTER 14

# *Persevere*

P*ersevere: continue in a course of action even in the face of difficulty or with little or no prospect of success.*[1]

The very definition of the word nearly sends chills down my spine. To carry on through the difficulty even when you are completely uncertain of the faintest possibility of success? This makes me want to scream, "What is the point?" According to God's word in James 1:4, it is so that we will lack nothing.

**James 1:4 / Let perseverance finish its work so that you may be mature and complete, not lacking anything. (NIV)**

Now one thing is quite clear from the word of God: we will face storms and trials of all kinds. When God leads you to the next stage or season of life, you will encounter challenges and setbacks because God doesn't want you lacking any good thing.

Something I love that Joyce Meyer said was, "One reason we must go through trials is to test our quality (see 1 Peter 4:12).

Often, we find ourselves wishing we had the faith of Sister so-and-so or Brother so-and-so. I can assure you, if they have a strong and vibrant faith, they did not develop it easily. Just as muscles are strengthened through exercise, firm faith comes from the furnace of affliction."[2] We are strengthened through perseverance, and being able to delay our instant gratification builds up our spiritual potency.

There have been many studies about the ability to delay gratification in order to reap a larger reward. One notable research project was done by Stanford professor Walter Mischel where he tested children on their ability to delay gratification using marshmallows. Children were given the opportunity to have one marshmallow treat right away or receive two if they were willing to wait for 15 minutes. They found astoundingly that the children who were able to wait demonstrated higher levels of success in all areas of life over the span of 40 years. They were able to handle stress better, had better health, had higher test scores, and demonstrated elevated social skills and status.[3]

Although this research is from a popular psychological study, I believe it is rooted in the biblical principle of perseverance. Having the ability to endure a situation and wait patiently on the promises of God will give us the necessary tools we need to have true success in all areas of life. Being able to delay our immediate desires builds character that helps us to finish strong.

Are you prepared to wait on God, even if that means that you might be waiting for awhile? Can you be content and patient with very slow, incremental movement? When God has given me direction and I make plans to follow, I get very impatient when things don't progress immediately. I have had to remind myself of how God creates a new life. He anoints a human embryo, and then takes nine months to grow and develop all the necessary systems that life will need to survive on the outside of the mother's womb. A human being is a magnificent creation and if it takes nine months, I should expect God's greatest gifts in my life to take time to develop.

Some delays will feel full of expectancy, like pregnancy, while others will seem mundane, like tax returns. Don't let the ordinary, lull-in-momentum cause you to doubt or abandon the call. Be patient, persevere, and trust. Trust in God's timing and trust in God's process. Be willing to endure the "changes in direction" and "divine delays," whether they are self-inflicted or circumstantial. We have all the tools we need to navigate well during any setbacks life presents.

### Headwinds

By definition, a headwind is a wind blowing from directly in front, opposing forward motion.[4] A strong headwind can delay our expected time of arrival, and possibly change the direction you are heading. I have experienced many types of headwinds in life, but I'd like to discuss three specific varieties which include: hurdles, circumstances, and distractions. All of which require perseverance to see it through.

All three can prevent us from moving forward. Some we have to leap over or step around, some we need to change perspective and generate new resources, while others will require discipline to bring back our focus. During our journey we will all be given the opportunity to overcome these headwinds in order to arrive at our planned destination. That is worth repeating: ALL of us will have the opportunity to overcome these headwinds. Be encouraged, however, because winds of any variety provide movement, and with proper preparation, wisdom, and courage, we can intentionally use the wind to drive us toward our God-given destiny, not away from it.

### CHAPTER 15

# *Hurdles*

In the traditional sense of a hurdle, we might imagine an athlete leaping over a wooden gate. A hurdle in the context of our spiritual journey will more likely be a problem we must overcome. Hurdles often require creativity and perseverance to solve. If we consider our sailors of old, they might have encountered a lack of clean drinking water, a shortage of edible food, or a lack of shelter from the elements .

A particular hurdle from my own life came when I finally got to attend New York University. I was living in southeast Missouri where I had grown up and had a full scholarship, but I was absolutely miserable. I longed to get out of my hometown for a long time and although I was going through the motions, I felt a strong lethargy in the pace moving forward.

I wasn't engaging in the kinds of opportunities I felt God had called me to seek out. I began to slip into a depression, and was on the verge of giving up on my dreams. My mother reached out to a close family friend who challenged me to follow my dream of moving to New York and studying acting. He helped me see that I wasn't stuck at all, if I didn't choose to be. I was waiting on life to proceed, but I wasn't taking any actions to turn my rudder in the direction of my dream. I had dropped anchor and was waiting on a change in my wind. He showed me that I must take the first step in faith toward my goal and be persistent. If I was going to be able to leap over the hurdle, I had to get some momentum.

After that conversation, I began applying to schools in the greater Manhattan area–for the second time. That tiny change in perception and direction triggered a shift in my natural and spiritual momentum. It was a matter of weeks when I got an invitation to do a study abroad at NYU for the spring term and I literally jumped for joy, feeling like I had won the lottery. NYU had been my dream school and I felt such a sense of peace that this was the next step in the journey. I said goodbye to the safety of living close to home and to all that I had known. I was finally embarking on the journey I had felt compelled toward from a very young age.

I was only a temporary student at NYU and I had to reapply for full admission, but eventually I was accepted as a full time student. However, there was one huge issue, which is a common hurdle for many of us: money.

NYU was nearly four times the expense that my state school was at home and I lost most of my scholarship, so I needed a few miracles in order to stay and study in New York. I distinctly remember sobbing to my parents about how I was going to be able to stay and finish my degree in New York.

At the time, neither of them were able to co-sign for a student loan, so I was pretty much on my own. It was like I was trying to sail across the ocean in a dingy. I didn't realize at the time God had already secured a larger vessel for me.

By God's grace and the generous giving of a personal friend, I was able to secure the funding I needed for the next term. This proceeded to happen two additional times before I was able to graduate. God only gave me what I needed for the next term; He made me get very comfortable with the uncertainty of where I might have to move next. He wanted me to keep moving, and trusting that no matter what the next hurdle was, it was well within His power to overcome it.

If you are facing a hurdle in your life, have you given that need over to the one who controls all things? You won't know where or how the need will be met, but God always provides for His children. If you are facing another type of hurdle, such as a need for physical healing, I would encourage you to place your faith in The Great Physician. Ask for Him to walk with you daily toward health.

When we face a hurdle on the journey, we must refocus our faith and our trust toward God. We might need to get some momentum and begin moving so God can guide us. If we set our hearts and minds on Him, God will provide a way around, over, or through the hurdle.

### CHAPTER 16

# A Change in Circumstances

Another headwind we can experience is a change in our circumstances. These often present themselves like a fork in the road. A decision must be made on how we are going to proceed. We must change our perspective and our plans in order to continue the journey. Circumstantial changes occur everyday.

I experienced a multi-layered change in circumstances when I was pregnant with both of my children. The change in circumstances specifically impacted my relationship with my mother-in-law.

When I first got married, I loved my mother-in-law, Chrissy; she was the best! (Honestly, I love her more today.) She lived on the east coast and we were on the west coast so we didn't see each other much, but we chatted on the phone often. We built a strong foundation, however it was a long distance relationship. The first change in circumstances occurred when Alex and I moved to the east coast. My mother-in-law and I had to work really hard to maintain and grow our love for each other. It was a bit like having a long distance friendship becoming a next door neighbor. You get to know more of their idiosyncrasies. Some were good, others were challenging.

As we were relearning our relationship roles, my health changed dramatically when I was put on bed rest with my second child. This was the second change in circumstances and I needed help. Chrissy came often to provide that assistance. I was grateful and resentful all at the same time. I felt smothered and I quickly realized we do things very differently. I wanted to be the one cooking meals for my family, I wanted things to be tidy, I wanted to make decisions about how to raise my daughter, but I was stuck on the couch without much choice in the matter. I was so resentful in my spirit. It wasn't anything specific that Chrissy was doing or saying; it was the fact that she had taken over. Out of necessity she had taken over the role of mom.

What I didn't realize was that she was praying without ceasing that we would have a strong and healthy relationship. I was young and impatient and extremely opinionated. I was not very good at asking for help, or allowing others to serve me, even when I needed it. Looking back, Jesus was helping knock some of the hard edges off of me by making me sit still and be served.

My circumstances went from absolute independence to complete dependence.

Over time I realized how selfless this woman was, how in love with my family she was, and how much she reflected the love of Jesus. I was taken aback by how she served without end. I fell totally in love with her heart and who she is.

Since that time and my subsequent repentance, we have built

an incredible relationship. In fact, she has attended every wedding in my immediate family; she made such an impact on all of us. God changed my perception in the circumstances to see Him at work in my life through her. I didn't understand it at the time, but once I surrendered my own pride, I was able to cultivate one of the most fruitful relationships in my journey.

My mother-in-law has single-handedly saved my marriage multiple times. I feel so loved and embraced by her that I bring even the most delicate topics to her.

Perhaps your circumstances are a bit more traumatic or heavy. Have you sustained a life-changing injury, lost a home or job, or maybe you are still waiting on a change? These types of circumstances can feel unbearable, crushing, overwhelming, and ruthless. When we are facing agonizing conditions, it is hard to see God at work.

I pray that if you are in a situation where your circumstances are preventing you from having peace, joy, or contentment, ask God to change your perspective. Ask for God goggles, and see if the sea will open up and show you something new. Here are a few prayer statements to get you started:

- God, help me see you at work through my circumstances.
- Give me divine perspective about my circumstances.
- Help me to overcome my circumstances in mind, body, and spirit.

Even when we face circumstances that seem impossible, God is able to do immeasurably more than we can ask or think.

**Ephesians 3:20 / God is able to do much more than we ask or think through His power working in us. (NLV)**

### CHAPTER 17

# Distraction

The last type of headwind I will talk about–although there are many more–is distraction. Can you imagine what would happen on a sailing ship if half of the crew were distracted by the beauty of the sea or the dazzle of the sunset? Ships keep moving and the work is constant. The crew must always be listening and alert, especially while on deck. There is a time to go below for rest, but when you are moving, distraction could mean death. This is one of the most common and insidious forces against our forward spiritual momentum. It is everywhere and in everything.

I cannot tell you the countless hours I have spent trolling Facebook, Instagram, and Pinterest in an effort to avoid writing this book. I am not a procrastinator by nature, but when I have a goal or vision that is God ordained, it seems that distraction is all around. I have found myself being distracted by laundry, cleaning the kitchen, busyness at work, and movie watching; oh, the movie watching. After a long day at work, feeding the kids, putting them to bed, and finally sitting down for the evening, the last thing I wanted to try and do was sit down at my computer again and write. As soon as I sat down my eyes would grow tired and I found myself asleep.

Overcoming distraction requires discipline. Discipline is the activity, exercise, or regimen that develops or improves a skill or training. It is often associated with punishment inflicted in order to create a set pattern of good behavior.

When we commit to following God's plan and we allow distraction to set in, we are disobeying. I always told my children that delayed obedience is still disobedience. It's kind of frightening to think that while we allow distractions to keep us from our calling, the enemy of our souls is enjoying the delay he created.

We can miss the boat altogether by allowing distraction to creep into our journey. This is why I say distraction is the most insidious of the headwinds described because most of the time they are "harmless" and even necessary for our lives to run smoothly.

The discrepancy lies when they take priority over doing the work of following the path. Distraction disobedience occurs when you knowingly choose an activity that delays your progress. It can be choosing to watch a movie when you know you should be writing. It can be sweeping the floors when you should be spending quality time with your husband. It can be sleeping too late everyday when you know God is asking you to meet with Him early in the morning. What are the common distractions that grab your attention? Maybe it's not a thing or a task, but a person. A common distraction which is easily overlooked is unfruitful relationships.

I wasted an epic amount of time in relationships that did nothing but move me further from God. Mostly these relationships were with men, but there were a few involving my girlfriends as well. I think when God is leading you to do something, you have to be ruthless in how you "trim the sails." This is such a sorry word pun, so I apologize for that, but it is a perfect analogy to tying back those relationships that are not helping you grow.

Before I met Alex, I was in a serious "friendship" with a man who neither wanted to call me his own or allow me to find someone who did. He was a master manipulator and treated me like a girlfriend behind closed doors but more like an acquaintance in public. I was heartbroken regularly by this disconnect in our relationship, but it was like an addiction. I wanted to feel accepted and honored by this man. I wanted him to see how valuable I was and to recognize that we could be an unstoppable force together.

Unfortunately, he never came around, and I caught him cheating on me with a woman that was almost 20 years my senior. It was a huge blow to my self confidence, and yet I continued to see this nitwit. He was a huge distraction in my life. I spent far too much time waiting for the scraps.

God wanted me to stop looking to this man for validation and start seeing God as the only one who can truly validate me. Once I did turn to God, the addictive nature of our relationship changed. The chains of needing that man to make me feel good about myself were severed. God never intended me to settle for table scraps; His vision was for me to come into His throne room and assume the role of princess. Yes, He designed me for royalty, but that calling isn't just for me; it is for all of us who choose His way.

I challenge you to evaluate all the relationships and activities that clamour for your attention during any given day or week. I understand there is so much vying for our attention and it can be difficult to eliminate some of the distractions, especially when they are fun distractions. The best question to ask yourself before you get caught up in another episode of your favorite program is: "How will I feel about how I used my time?" If the activities you choose to give your time to bring you closer to what God has planned for you, you will feel fulfilled.

Equally important is being very critical about whether or not our relationships are honoring our Father. Would you be able to say that your relationships are drawing you closer to the plans God has prepared? In other words, do the people in your circle of friends and family encourage you or distract you? Let's be ruthless in eliminating distractions so that we can be alert, and ready to "trim our sails" at any moment.

Questions to Consider:

- What relationships or activities distract me?
- How would I feel if I eliminated some of these distractions?
- How can I refocus when I know I have given into distraction?

Of all the headwinds described, which ones are you currently facing? I encourage you to get some momentum if it is a hurdle, ask for a perspective change if it is circumstances, and "trim your sails" if it is distractions. Remind yourself that you have all you need to overcome every headwind life blows your way.

### CHAPTER 18

# Deep Water

I will need to provide a little bit of context for this particular navigational problem. When I refer to deep water, I am referring to when you are way out to sea and no longer see the shoreline. All of the familiar landmarks are gone and you are left to trust you are moving in the right direction given your last-known course heading.

I equate this to the times in our journey where God goes radio silent. That awful moment as you are cruising along and getting all kinds of feedback and then suddenly you cannot see or hear any of the familiar markings telling you that you were on the right track. This particular situation has presented itself in my journey so often, and I can honestly say it has not gotten much easier. I feel completely confident doing things a bit differently or risking beyond what the world views as prudent, so long as I can hear from the Lord and He continues to confirm moment by moment that I'm doing the right thing. However, God doesn't babysit us to follow through with His vision. He leaves the trusting in faith part up to us.

That doesn't change the fact that seasons of limbo and uncertainty are hard.

Even though I hadn't envisioned I would become a writer, speaker, or teacher of the Gospel, people began professing this over my life. Close friends would say things like:"I was watching Beth Moore the other day and I couldn't help but see you," or "I was really struggling the other day but then I thought, 'what would Mama Carey do?' and I actually got brave and did it!" or "You will be on that platform someday and you will look behind you and see an amazing ministry you built".

Hearing these kinds of encouraging words made me believe I was being called to ministry. I investigated Bible college with a specific interest in old testament culture and history. I was hopeful that I would someday work for church.

However, outside of these powerful words, there were no signs indicating this would be the case. In fact, often times it felt the opposite, as though I would never become what these people had been saying of me. After all, I began working in higher education far from ministry in the traditional sense. If I am honest, in some ways, I felt a bit abandoned. I would ask myself, "Where are you, God? What was all that about? I didn't ask for that." Once I started to get excited about the possibility, it seemed everything came to a slow crawl.

Regardless of how I feel, God was and is unchanging. We are the ones that move in and out of a deep relationship with Him. So rather than asking "Where are you, God?," a better question is, "Where did I drift off course? Show me what I need to repent of? What should I do now?"

In this feeling of limbo, I needed to pull myself away from my busy life and spend time with the Lord and give Him my undivided attention. I needed to search my life for anything that was blocking my ability to hear from God.

Many people take a yearly sabbatical for this precise reason. It can take so many forms, but often times it is three to seven days in a secluded spot without much access to the outside world, armed with a notebook/laptop, a Bible, and a willingness to worship, seek, and repent. In lieu of going away, you can and should pull yourself away for a few hours to pray and read the word. Listen carefully to what God has to say.

Ask specific questions like:

- Where did I stop listening to you, Lord?
- Why don't I hear from you now?
- Is there anything I need to repent of?

In my quiet reflection time, I discovered I needed forgiveness.

I was struggling with this job I loathed. Working in that environment everyday made me not like people. I was so wiped out from this season of trying to contact, help, and meet the needs of some very demanding individuals. I was ready to move to Antarctica and never have a conversation with a human again. I started to dislike who I was becoming. I realized I needed a change.

Rather than ask the Lord, I begged Alex to let me quit. He was adamant that I had a "good job" and needed to stick with it. So not only did this job make me dislike people, but it was also causing a divide in my marriage! YIKES!

Clearly I had drifted off course somewhere along the lines. God specifically called me to this battlefield and I was failing miserably.

I locked myself in my prayer closet and cried out to the Lord for help. "Release me from this!" I moaned. I prayed for months without any signs or shifts in the situation. I started looking for other opportunities hoping Alex would give me permission to move on. I found another job that met all the benchmarks I was looking for and asked Alex if I could quit now. He still said no.

At this point, I literally felt like God and Alex didn't care about my health or well-being, and they were just being mean by making me stay in the situation. I prayed to God again: "Lord, what should I do?" He answered, "Stay in your job."

Ugh.

I regret to admit, I was a whining child in that moment. I then felt God leading me to examine my timeline and my personal goals. I did so and asked myself a critical question: "Can I endure this job if I know that it is not forever?" The resounding feeling was yes.

### Philippians 4:13 / I can do all things through Christ who strengthens me. (NKJV)[1]

I recognized that I was throwing a fit because of the pain I was having to endure. I asked Jesus to forgive my poor attitude. After all, He endured the cross. Here I was, thinking I would be great at helping grow God's church, when I wasn't spiritually mature enough to love people that were hard to love. It was pitiful. It was in that revelation of my need for forgiveness that I resolved myself to obey despite my feelings about the job.

Shortly after my repentance, I had to attend a national sales meeting. I had the opportunity to minister to a young man on my team who was struggling with his identity. He had been raised in a Christian family and had always followed the "Christian rules," but had a lot of insecurities bubbling under the surface that had never been brought to light. There were many tensions between him and his family and he felt rejected by those nearest and dearest to him.

My heart broke for this incredible man that was trying to follow God and felt lost, hurt, and abandoned. In that exchange, God revealed to me that this was the church He had chosen for me for the time being.

God elaborated further and said that my ministry begins with the communities and environments He sets before me. I longed to have the safety of serving in the church, where I had permission to speak into the spiritual lives of people. I never thought I would have to be courageous enough to pray for people who were agnostic, atheist, and backslidden.

I returned home feeling quite unworthy of the responsibility. Inadequate to overcome my own vanity and selfishness. A true humbling of my spirit had occurred and it was so refreshing to be reminded that my Creator is in control. He has the perfect plan. My vision might not always align with God's, but His is always bigger and better than I could imagine. While I was feeling lost, abandoned, and confused, God remained right where He always had been, waiting for me to ask, "Where to next? Who can I serve today?"

If you find yourself in that uncomfortable situation where you haven't heard from God in a while, He is waiting. Don't let the radio silence or lack of future landmarks fool you into thinking God isn't there or no longer cares. He is, and will always be ready to speak into your life and provide you with the next steps.

Quiet your spirit and humble yourself, re-commit to prayer, ask for forgiveness, and seek God's direction. In the stillness of your heart, your Heavenly Father is whispering His plans for you in every moment.

Just like sailors measured where they were based on when they last had evidence of location, we have to lean in to God's voice and trust that our last word was accurate and the next one is already firmly found in our future.

### CHAPTER 19

# *You Run Aground*

We all have accounts where we have hastily moved forward in a situation without calculating the full repercussions of those actions. Equally true are events that literally stop us in our tracks and rapidly change the course of our direction. Either one of these I associate with running aground. There is a saying in the world of sailing that states, "If you haven't run aground you haven't been around."[1]

This holds true in life as well. If you have never experienced a dramatic slowing or complete halting of your forward momentum, you probably haven't truly lived. It is likely that you have played it safe, "spiritually speaking," and not fully risked to the limits of yourself and your faith in God. Let me first note that running aground is not necessarily an indication that you are off course. While I do believe that God doesn't necessarily want us to crash, sometimes that might be the best way to empower and equip us in that moment. Just think for a moment: how it might feel to run aground?

If we are talking real navigational situations, you would hope it is a soft grounding in mud or sand. These types of minor crashes create the least amount of damage and typically only delay your arrival. These opportunities might just call for a time to wait for the tide to come in and lift us out of the mud or sand. However, there are also groundings that occur on rocky reefs that can create so much devastation you must abandon ship. In those moments, you might feel upset, hopelessness, fear, desperation, or uncertainty. Your intended destination will feel further away than ever. Either way you look at it, running aground is an indefinite delay in your progress toward your destination.

Running aground can take many forms, such as a car accident, a sudden illness, or it can be the loss of a place to live or a loved one. No matter the form, this will take a completely new approach to reset and get back on course. When you run aground while sailing, an evaluation of the damage is the first thing that must be done. Rather than freaking out and automatically abandoning ship, you will need to take an honest evaluation of how bad the damage is. Oftentimes the enemy to our spirit will exaggerate the reality in an effort to get us to make hasty decisions and cause even further unnecessary delays or destruction.

As I mentioned previously, I was trained in the dramatic arts, so I have a big tendency to over-dramatize a situation. Thankfully, I married a man who has no time for drama and immediately nips my exaggeration in the proverbial rear end. I admit that when this happens in the moment I am not always calmly responsive. My dramatic personality is more akin to the style of Chicken Little: "The sky is falling!" I have recognized this about myself and know that when I encounter a dramatic slowing of progress, it is time for me to have honest and sober judgment. I personally have to ask people that love and care about me to help in these circumstances.

One of those people is Alex, but my dad is also one of those people. My dad is not a man of many words but he is a man of wisdom. When I have encountered great difficulty I can rely on him to provide sound advice, laced with a heavy dose of love and care for me and my family. You see my dad has experienced groundings of every variety and has successfully navigated each one. My dad studies the word of God, he goes on sabbatical once a year, and he trains his mind to capture negative thinking. I have watched him endure some of the most painful circumstances and continue to extend grace. This is why I trust his advice.

When you run aground in life, seek wisdom from those who you respect and are not emotionally volatile, who can offer a perspective from outside the situation.

If we are to arrive at our destination according to God's will, we must build up a crew. God is the captain who gives the orders of where we ought to go next, and we are like the first mate. We are second-in-command of our own lives.

However, the larger your ship becomes, the more likely you will need a crew to safely navigate the waters of life. When you are young and single and just setting out, you are in the equivalent of a small dingy. Don't discount your little boat because you are moving forward and you are very agile. You hear God's call and you can immediately head in that direction. As you grow in life, however, you begin to expand not just your boat, but your community influence, and all of a sudden your tiny dingy has grown as well. This means that turning or changing directions quickly requires us to include others in helping us.

A key in life to get back on course after you run aground is to seek the counsel of wise men and women. These people can be your Pastor or a qualified Christian counselor. This group can include trusted friends and relatives; we need to open ourselves up to those people we respect to hold us accountable for our choices, both good and bad. When you feel that you have run aground, think about people you trust. These are not just people you trust to keep a secret, but you also trust them to tell you the truth about yourself. These people will become your crew that holds you accountable to the call on your life.

Make sure that the people you are seeking wisdom from exhibit the habits of a mature believer, and that their own lives are "bearing fruit." What I mean by that is, do they read the word regularly, do they have solid friendships, are they respected in their communities, have you seen them demonstrate integrity?

## A Soft Grounding

So often the Lord has spoken to me through those that are closest to me, like my sister or my husband, or even my own children. I experienced a soft grounding when I had had a particularly long day and my patience was nil. I came home from work already exhausted and frustrated.

I felt like I was in one of those TV sitcoms where the Dad comes home and kicks the dog because he just got beat down by the day. I didn't have a dog at the time, so my kiddos bore the brunt of my bad day. I was incredibly short, and when they began to bicker when I asked them to do a chore to help me, I stormed around the house and did the chores myself. I didn't yell, but the kids clearly knew I was not in a mood that was prepared to be loving and understanding. Later that night when I was tucking them in bed, I had to ask for forgiveness, as I have to do more often than I would like to admit.

At any rate, my daughter said, "It's ok, Mommy, I'm sorry you had a hard day today." I thought that was the end of it, but after I had gone back downstairs and cleaned the house up and then proceeded to put myself to bed, a letter was on my nightstand. It had all the markings of a handwritten and decorated letter of a nine-year-old little girl, including purple marker ink. The words that she had taken so much time to write were nothing short of the voice of God himself. They went something along the lines of, "Mommy, I love you, Daddy loves you, your friends love you. Some things I like about you are that you are funny, adventurous, nice (most of the time) and smart."

She reminded me of who I am called to be and how much I am loved, no matter what the day put on me. All this to say, I had run aground in life that day. When we get stuck in the mud or sand, sometimes we just need to wait for the tide to change. Sometimes in our spiritual journey we need to wait for the Holy Spirit to fill us and lift us up. If you feel that your momentum has slowed to a crawl or completely stopped, ask the Holy Spirit to fill you up. Let God's countenance lift your spirit and may you sing praises even in the slow times.

### Dashed on the Rocks— *What to do when your boat breaks.*

Sometimes our "grounded" moments are moments and other times they are full on crashes that take time to rebuild. What if your situation is the equivalent of smashing against the rocks and destroying the boat altogether? What do you do when you are devastated? I know that when I have felt this way I didn't know what to do and I felt quite helpless. The enemy is always right beside you in that moment, feeding you lies: "Did I hear God right? How could He do this to me? I thought He loved me?"

Be on your guard in these situations because as a strong believer in the goodness of my heavenly Father, if you have been leaning into God's voice and the truth found in His word, you are right where He intended you to be—even if at the moment you feel as if you are floating on a piece of your broken ship in the middle of the ocean.

As I was researching this chapter I was trying to work out an answer to the following questions: why we do crash in life? God is good, right? He loves us and doesn't want us to smash against the rocks, right? So why would people experience these life shattering situations where they literally come to a sudden and painful stop? What I felt in my spirit was: "Sometimes I have to teach you how to build a bigger boat. Sometimes my intentions for a person are much larger than they can see. I want them to lack no good thing and therefore I must teach them to rebuild from the inside out." I was shocked, and felt so much comfort in those words.

God wants us to be so equipped we can quite literally build the boat we need to move forward. That does not diminish the pain or fear we might feel in that moment, but it certainly takes a bad situation and transforms it into an opportunity. I don't want to diminish the very real fear, anger, and rage that sometimes accompanies a life crisis. So many are struggling not to drown, so please know that if you are treading water at the moment, the Creator of the Universe is there with you, breathing new life moment by moment, strengthening your legs to keep you floating along until He brings you to shore.

Sometimes we run aground and crash because we are in the wrong kind of boat. Maybe we get really comfortable in our little dingy. However, God needs us to build a sailboat, or maybe even a cruise ship. After having this revelation, many of my destructive crashes in life made a lot more sense. Hindsight is often 20/20. Painful and abusive relationships that came to a halt crushed me in the moment but helped me build a stronger boat. The next boat had no room for crew members who didn't have my best interests at heart.

My sister has a large blended family of six amazing children. When she got married she inherited two bonus children whom she had known and loved from the tender ages of two and five. She and my brother-in-law had been married only a year when his sister got very sick. My sister's sister-in-law was diagnosed with terminal brain cancer. It grew so fast and she deteriorated quickly. During all of this, my sister became pregnant with their first child, so her life became like a made-for-TV movie. At any rate, my sister cooked, cleaned, and cared for her new family during this time and did her best to support her husband as he did a lot of the heavy lifting in the family dynamic as his sister finally went home to be with Jesus. When she did, she left her adopted son William to the care of her brother and my sister. He became the third child in my sister's tribe. My sister stayed faithful and built a bigger boat.

Rough and rocky times came when the oldest daughter went to live more permanently with her mom. It was shattering to both my sister and my brother-in-law, as they had spent so much time and effort in raising her during her formative years. All this began as number five and six made their arrivals. Even though it was a very difficult season, God was faithful to them in finance and in patience with their tribe. He led them and continues to guide them on how to parent and direct each child in the way they should go. It is a daily struggle that they are continuing to bear, but I love what they named their ranch in Nebraska: Mended Fences Acres.

God broke something inside each one of them, but is building something bigger, lasting, and absolutely beautiful.

I want to reiterate again that I am under no delusions this story is the same level of pain or devastation some of you have navigated. Some of you have circumstances you are facing right now that involve tragic grief, financial ruin, or a looming hopelessness for which you might not see an end in sight. However, I pray that you will be encouraged that God's promises don't intend for us to stay in this place forever. His joy and peace and glory are just beyond the horizon.

### Psalm 30:5 / Weeping may endure for a night, but joy comes in the morning. (NKJV)

Regardless of how you were grounded, we will need to have a crew to help remind us of who we are and where we are headed. They will be the ones to help show us how to rebuild and to cheer us on as we persevere. Seek wisdom and be open to correction no matter where it might come from, and be humble enough to accept help when you need it. Humility leads to restoration in so many ways.

### Proverbs 11:2 / Pride leads to disgrace, but with humility comes wisdom. (NLT)

### CHAPTER 20

# A Storm Rises

In light of the last segment about running aground, sometimes these are caused by a storm rising in our lives. The interesting thing about literal storms is that usually we can see a storm coming. We sense there is change heading our way and we take cover. If we are sensitive to the Holy Spirit moving in our lives, He is faithful to prepare us for a storm. I have found that those inclinations have helped me to safeguard my mind, my emotions, my family, and my marriage during a season of facing life's storms.

There are several sailing tactics used in navigating a storm and, depending on where you are, you either find a safe harbour and take anchor, or you head out into the open water and get enough sea room between you and the shoreline so that you will not crash into any shallow land formations.[1] Either way you approach, necessary precautions are taken and decisions are made to give the boat and crew the best possible chance of "weathering" the storm. The definition of weathering is to be able to endure or successfully deal with a very difficult problem.[2] Again, we must be willing to persevere.

Wouldn't I love to say that when I have encountered difficult problems, I simply trimmed the sails, heaved to the wind, and rode out the storm with grace and faith. I hope this comes as an encouragement to you that I did not. Even though I sensed the pending storm and I prepared mentally for the transitions, I have failed over and over in my stormy seasons.

A recent example is when Alex got a new job that required him to travel a lot. We are talking about 75% or more during the week; every week he was gone and I was left at home with the kids and everything that we normally shared responsibility for were solely on my shoulders. Now, we both knew this was going to be a change and we prayerfully accepted this position; however, once this new pattern was upon us I did not weather the change well. I hypothetically saw the clouds of life begin to change and warn me of the coming challenges, and yet I still scrambled to find peace and refuge. It wasn't until several months of fighting the feelings of abandonment, loneliness, and bitterness that I realized I needed a plan. I needed God to help me put together a strategy to weather this storm. It took me surrendering my own ability to find a way to keep my marriage strong, and giving that huge responsibility over to God.

During a storm it is critical to prioritize what is most important. When we just stand on the bow while the waves threaten to topple our ship with every rise and fall, and we don't bother to trim the sail or turn ourselves in such a way that we can endure, we can expect the storm to do more damage. Instead, we partner with God during our storms to strengthen us, our ship, and for Him to control the wind and waves.

**Matthew 8:27 / The men were amazed and asked, "What kind of man is this? Even the winds and the waves obey him!" (NIV)**

This is only one of many examples in the word of God about who controls the ocean, both literally and figuratively. I would encourage you if you are currently riding out a storm to go and read a few of the following passages and ask yourself, "Can I trust the God who commands the earth, sea and sky?"

> Matthew 8:25-28
> Psalm 89:9
> Psalm 95:5-6
> Proverbs 30:4-5
> Jeremiah 5: 22
> Exodus 14: 27-28

I'll admit that during another storm in life, I didn't sit with God and remain calm as He led me to safety. I panicked and even my prayers were not those full of faith but terror-stricken pleas for help. I was begging for help and not seeing that during the storm, God was right there "asleep on my boat."

**Mark 4:37-39 / A furious squall came up, and the waves broke over the boat, so that it was nearly swamped. Jesus was in the stern, sleeping on a cushion. The disciples woke him and said to him, "Teacher, don't you care if we drown?" He got up, rebuked the wind and said to the waves, "Quiet! Be Still!" Then the wind died down and it was completely calm. (NIV)**

During this particularly stormy season, when Alex and I were unsure of when our next paycheck would come, I would wake up in the middle of the night and place myself on the hard, cold floor begging for God to rescue us from this uncertainty. While it is spiritually good to recognize our place in front of the most High God, I was doing it more out of guilt. Inside I was trying to manipulate God: "See Lord, how I am punishing myself and humbling myself. . . I am nothing, I am drivel, please pick me up." I imagined Jesus looking down at me like a good father and thinking to himself, "Wow, that is a beautiful tantrum."

I had a wonderful mentor at this time (a fabulous member of my crew) who I called and pleaded with to help me pray and understand God during this storm. She was so courageous and had lived as a missionary for over 30 years with three children along for the ride. She told me countless stories of how she had only change in her pocket; she once had to plug a wall heater with coins to keep their tiny apartment warm. In this moment of my own storm, I wanted to understand how she was able to endure that uncertainty. How could you possibly get through that, stay happily married, and raise three incredible children who are astoundingly successful today? She admitted during that time she felt a lot like me, and asked the same questions of God. Namely, why are you not rescuing us? The words she spoke to me next convicted my spirit so much so that it continues to resonate in my head today and in every storm: "Stop praying these panicked, whining, wimpy prayers. You either trust God is sovereign, all powerful, and loves you. . . or you don't. Start trusting and praying prayers of faith in the promises and vision God has presented to you."

WOAH! I either believed in God's promises or I didn't. Keep in mind I had been a Christian for many years already and I was faithfully in church every Sunday, but I was not fully trusting in God. This is where I recognized I had made financial security my idol. God allowed a storm to pluck that demi-god from my heart.

Even though I still struggle with the idol of security creeping back in, I pray more powerfully than I ever have. The storm did what it was intended to do: remove an idol from my mind, strengthen my faith, and increase my ability to believe in the miraculous.

Fast forward in life to a new storm with different challenges. I don't always get it right, but I can tell you that it gets easier to recognize when I haven't been allowing God to command the wind and waves.

In the case of the storm of relentless travel, the first few weeks when Alex began traveling a lot, I lost my temper with my kids multiple times. I felt exhausted and overwhelmed. Lastly, I put on my "single mom" trousers and tried to do life in my own strength. The storm clouds were large, heavy with rain, and full of angry thunder and lighting. After a few long weeks and my patience hanging by a thread, I went to Alex and asked, "When is this going to get better?" He promised it was only going to be the first few months while he got to know the team and the territory better. Again, I was only thinking about tactics for survival in the short term, not believing I could endure anything with Christ.

I recognized within about two months that this wasn't going to "get better," and if anything, it might get worse and continue for the duration of this job. I needed a better plan and a more realistic tactic to weather this storm. Several things happened: I began praying for peace and direction from God. I also prayed for Him to release me from my job so I had less responsibilities in that area. I was praying for alleviation of the storm.

Unfortunately, that was not God's plan.

I was at my wits end and ready to quit my job even though I felt in my heart it was not yet the time. I finally took my husband's advice, as well as a close friend, to change my work schedule to accommodate my life. I took my work email off of my phone so that I wasn't constantly being pulled back to my computer and feeling unable to engage my kids wholeheartedly. I also shut off from work at 6pm every night so I could spend time with my family and catch up on the household chores. God made me realize in this storm that "completing all the tasks" didn't make me a better person, employee, wife, or mom. God reminded me to "Do only that which I have set out for today." What a relief.

I can testify that this storm endured for longer than I had hoped, but my sails were trimmed up and it caused me to turn back toward the goals that I feel God laid out for me.

I am not going to pretend that this example is a category five hurricane, but it certainly is something that can shake your foundation. Perhaps you are going through a storm that has hurricane force winds or tsunami size waves. What do you do during these times of complete disruption, compared to a spring thunderstorm?

To be incredibly pragmatic, you do the same thing. You see the storm coming and prepare for what is on the horizon. An overly simplified analogy is to put on your raincoat and wellies. You wouldn't go to Antarctica without a heavy duty winter coat, and you wouldn't sail out into the open waters without equally "weatherproof" apparel.

God's word tells us to put on the armor of God.

### CHAPTER 21

# *Storm Gear*

As we see a storm approaching or find ourselves in the middle of a downpour, we should have some solid storm gear handy. Sailors have different gear they wear and use during a storm as compared to fair weather sailing. In Ephesians the Bible tells us about putting on the armor of God. I believe that if we want to weather storms well, we need to explore how putting on His armor can help.

> **Ephesians 6: 10-18 / ¹⁰Finally, be strong in the Lord and in his mighty power. ¹¹Put on the full armor of God, so that you can take your stand against the devil's schemes. ¹²For our struggle is not against flesh and blood, but against the rulers, against the authorities, against the powers of this dark world and against the spiritual forces of evil in the heavenly realms. ¹³Therefore put on the full armor of God, so that when**

**the day of evil comes, you may be able to stand your ground, and after you have done everything, to stand. ¹⁴Stand firm then, with the belt of truth buckled around your waist, with the breastplate of righteousness in place, ¹⁵and with your feet fitted with the readiness that comes from the gospel of peace. ¹⁶In addition to all this, take up the shield of faith, with which you can extinguish all the flaming arrows of the evil one. ¹⁷Take the helmet of salvation and the sword of the Spirit, which is the word of God. ¹⁸And pray in the Spirit on all occasions with all kinds of prayers and requests. With this in mind, be alert and always keep on praying for all the Lord's people. (NIV)**

This scripture speaks to me about preparedness for the day of trouble. In your storm, are you equipped with some armor? I am not a biblical theologian, so this is a disclaimer that this is my own take on how the different pieces of armor described can be defined and applied.

### Belt of truth

From the letter to the Ephesians, the author Paul is writing about an analogy between God's armor and that of a Roman soldier. The belt was a foundational element of armor that anchored other key pieces, including the sword. When we are discussing the belt of truth as it relates to our spiritual journey, it is referring to the word of Truth. In other words, God's truth found in scripture. This is your spiritual anchor in a storm; all the rest of the gear will hinge on this truth. Storms have a tendency to distract us, stir doubt, and create uncertainty. The scriptures, the gospel of truth, and the person of Jesus will provide a solid reference point for what the truth is during turbulent times.

The term "belt of truth" also reminds us to be truthful. Maybe you have been pretending, manipulative, or not completely honest with yourself or with God? Untruths are not from the Lord, they are from the enemy. Lies produce more lies, and lead to destruction.

Maybe you haven't admitted that you are terrified, you don't really believe God will help you, or you have given up hope. When the storm clouds gather, it isn't the time to hide it's time to get real. . . real quick. God's word will help free you from the fear of telling the truth in tough situations. Speaking the truth brings freedom, it brings peace, and it brings righteousness. There is no time in a storm to delay expressing the truth. The truth about how we feel about what we have done and what we are thinking of doing.

When we admit the truth, we are then positioned for the message of Jesus to strengthen us, convict us, and help us persevere through the storm.

### Breastplate of righteousness

Righteousness, by definition, is to behave in a moral and ethical way. It is to do what is right in God's eyes. According to God's word, being righteous affords us some divine protections during the storms and battles we may face.

**Proverbs 11:4 / Wealth is worthless in the day of wrath, but righteousness delivers from death. (NIV)**

I love this scripture because I think it highlights that wealth often tempts us to be unrighteous. Have you ever had an experience where you went out to dinner with a group and the bill came and everyone contributed the same amount but the check still came up short? I'm sure you know of someone who gets paid in cash and doesn't claim all the income on their taxes. This is a tiny way that unrighteousness can creep into our lives.

Finances are not the only area where the lines blur with regards to being righteous. What about our relationships to the opposite sex? A friendly or flirtatious conversation with a colleague doesn't really hurt anyone, right? The question is not whether something is harmful to another, it is whether or not the behavior would be considered righteous. Would you cheat on your taxes if you knew you were going to be audited? Would you flirt with that coworker if your spouse were able to see you?

Being righteous requires obedience to God's commandments. While there are more than 613 Mosaic laws, we are fortunate that Jesus summed up all the laws of God and the prophets beautifully into two commands:

**Luke 10:27 / Love the Lord your God with all your heart and with all your soul and with all your strength and with all your mind, and Love your neighbor as yourself. (NIV)**

What that means for me is that when I am in a storm or see one coming, I need to check whether I am acting with righteousness. At work? In my relationships? In my finances? Am I loving God with all my heart and my neighbor as myself? Don't drown in the upcoming storm because you were reluctant to take the high ground of righteous living.

### Readiness Shoes of the gospel of peace

Gospel translated means good news, so the gospel of peace must mean "good news of peace." Are we ready to share the good news of peace as we face a storm? Let us be expectant that God is going to work through us and in us during the storm. Could we possibly look at those rolling storm clouds as an opportunity for God to use us powerfully to demonstrate His faithfulness, His compassion, and His rescuing power?

Even though Paul knew he might be killed when he traveled to Jerusalem, he was ready. He was prepared to share the good news, even if that meant death. He steeped himself in the gospel of peace and was ready to face anything and share what he had found through Jesus. We are called to the same mission, to share our good news. When we see storm clouds rolling in, look for chances to share your good news.

**John 14:27 / Peace I leave with you, My peace I give to you; not as the world gives do I give to you. Let not your heart be troubled, neither let it be afraid. (NIV)**

Let's change the script of the impending storm that brings fear, dread, sorrow, or pain to the storm that brings an opportunity for God to do miraculous work through us. This mental adjustment can help us start looking for God's hand at work in our lives. When we recognize that this storm is part of our education, part of our journey, and part of others getting to know Jesus better, we can look at those storm's clouds as rain bringers, flower flourishers, and reservoir toppers, not just flood makers.

Do not become complacent or lazy during this time when it is so easy to give up. Storms are hard, and we grow weary very quickly when our physical, mental, and emotional bodies have struggled for a time. This is when we must remind ourselves who has called us to this journey. Be intentional about looking for God at work, and stay alert. God could call you to move and share your good news at a moments notice!

### *Shield of faith*

Putting our faith in God, in His promises, in the truth of His word, and the resurrection of Jesus will shield us. We must "take it up" to extinguish the flaming arrows of the enemy.

The darts of the enemy are sent from a distance and are meant to catch the target off guard. They can come in the form of sinful thoughts, strong temptations, and emotional outbursts. If we find ourselves in a storm and we are being tempted into sin, it is time to evaluate our faith. Who are we listening to? Who are we trusting?

I have often struggled with faith that felt like a hollow shell. It wasn't strong enough to withstand great trials. Early in my journey, my faith was weak because I believed that God could deliver me from certain things, but not others. I limited God's promises and power to things that specifically related to what I believed was spiritual. I trusted God with "church" stuff. My "life" stuff was my responsibility. Faith isn't limited or compartmentalized; it is a shield for your whole life.

Faith is believing or having confidence in something before you can actually see it.

**Hebrews 11:1 / Now faith is confidence in what we hope for and assurance about what we do not see. (NIV)**

Encourage yourself to believe in the almighty power and promises of God. I challenge you to make a choice during your storm to put all your trust in God.

Believe in healing before you are healed. Believe for resources before you have a job or money in the bank. Believe for restoration in relationships even when there is no indication of peace. God has promised that He will release healing, provision, opportunity, restoration, and resources to protect you and make you whole again.

## Helmet of Salvation

We wear helmets to protect our heads. This is due to the fact that injuries sustained to our head are often life-threatening and irreversible. The "helmet of salvation" protects us from any deathblow.

Salvation is a free gift of forgiveness and deliverance from our sins. It gives us the gift of eternal life. Just like a helmet can save a cyclist's life in an accident, our salvation saves us from sin and death! If you have not fully committed your life to serving Jesus and are facing a storm without a helmet, call out to Jesus and confess the following statement:

> *Jesus, I don't want to do life my way. I want to follow you and know you. Please forgive me of all the sins I have committed and help me forgive those who have hurt me, too. I believe you are Lord of all, and that you died on the cross for me and rose from the dead so that I might have eternal life. I surrender my life to you today; help me to follow you.*

For those of us who might have said that prayer, or a version of it, recently or many years ago, I would recommend reflecting on the gift of salvation. Sometimes reflecting on the mere thought of who we once were and who we are now can turn the tide of a raging storm. When we reflect on the gift of salvation it can impact the thoughts of our minds where the battle is lost and won, moment by precious moment.

### *Sword of the Spirit*

The only aspect of the armor that isn't primarily a defensive piece of equipment is the sword. Swords are used for both offense and defense. In the same way, scripture can be applied both offensively and defensively.

In the middle of a hurricane you will want everything available to you, especially the word of God. This is the best weapon against everything you will encounter in life. Even Jesus himself used the word of God as a weapon against the temptations of the enemy. Read **Matthew 4:1-11**. After Jesus fasted for forty days and forty nights, he was tempted.

I don't know about you, but if I hadn't eaten for forty days I think I would jump at any opportunity to fill my belly. I have only ever fasted for about five days and I thought I was going to die! Regardless of my limitations, Jesus was starving at this point. The first thing the enemy tempted him with? Food, of course! Jesus took out his sword and said,

**Matthew 4:4 / Man does not live on bread alone, but on every word that comes from the mouth of God. (NIV)**

This is very interesting for two reasons: when we are talking about the sword of the Spirit, not only does Jesus use the word against the temptation, but he also makes an outrageous claim: "I live on every word that comes from the mouth of God." Even the very feeling of being satiated comes from the word of God.

During a storm you need to live, breathe, sleep, and dream the word of God. Are you starving? Hungry for something new? Are you in desperate need of rescue? Ask God to reveal to you the weapon in His word that will help you to overcome and carry on.

In the middle of the storm when the waves are crashing over

your boat, when you feel that you are drowning, when you have lost all hope that you will make it through and feel you will never end up at your destination, put on the armor of God.

When sailors got tossed and turned around in a bad storm, they would oftentimes have to wait until the sun rose to determine which way they had drifted and what direction they were headed.

Let me challenge you in your storm: if you don't know which way you are going or where you are, let the SON rise in you. Let Jesus take the helm and be your anchor in the storm. Read His truth, speak His truth, do what is right, share the gospel message, strengthen your faith, reflect on your salvation, and apply the word of God to every situation. If you have put on the armor of God, you are likely in a very good position to weather the storms of life.

### CHAPTER 22

# *Additional Storm Survival Tips*

In addition to putting on the armor of God here are a few more practices we can implement in our lives to help us persevere through rough waters.

*Pray without ceasing*

## 1 Thessalonians 5:17 / Pray without ceasing (NKJV)

This can feel overwhelming if you have limited time. Filling our lives with stuff, appointments, and busyness is a tactic of the enemy. It prevents us from reaping the benefits and blessings of continuous prayer. Praying without ceasing just means that you pray small prayers all the time! You don't need to set aside massive chunks of time to do this; you just need to continually talk to God about your life. Prayer is a conversation between you and God.

There is a significant value in longer prayer sessions, but start by trying to have an ongoing chat with God. I pray prayers like, "Help that man or woman. Lead my children today. Give me wisdom at work. Help me be bold with a friend. Give me words to speak during this meeting." They are short, clear, and they keep my mind focused on God's will in my life. I also spend time each morning in a quiet space to pray. This helps me align my thoughts with God's first thing in the morning. I cherish this time with God and when I have missed a few mornings in a row, I have a longing to get back to my quiet prayer time. Not every morning brings a profound revelation, but it is always time well spent.

We all have the ability to continually converse with the King of Kings.

To put this in perspective, imagine for a moment that the Queen of England sent you a message and asked you to visit her. What if the only time the Queen could meet was at five in the morning? Wouldn't you get up earlier just so you were ready to meet her? Our invitation to meet with the Creator of the Universe is ongoing. He has an "open court" policy!

When we commit ourselves to prayer, we are spiritually approaching the throne of God the Father. It is a humbling thought. The King of Kings, the One True God, the Creator of the Universe, and the One who can bring about real change in our lives has an open invitation to speak to Him directly. He desires this constant communion with you.

I encourage you to begin to make prayer a consistent part of your daily dialogue. Ask God questions. Talk to Him about your fears, your doubts, and your dreams. Turn your eyes and heart to those around you and submit prayers on their behalf. You will begin to see that God is listening and answering you.

### *Be in community with other believers*

If you are in a rough storm you need other people to help carry the burden. This goes back a few chapters about building a crew, and they are more important than ever during storms. If you feel isolated and alone, it is time to engage with a group that can support you. The enemy of our souls wants us to believe we are the only ones experiencing loneliness, grief, loss, or pain. A good way to get plugged into a group is to commit to volunteer to serve others. It is one of the quickest ways to turn your sorrow to joy, when you serve those around you. *"I complained that I had no shoes until I met a man who had no feet."* –Persian proverb[1]

Find people around you that you can encourage and uplift.

This can prove to be a painful exercise in some instances because there will be people that complain about their seemingly perfect lives. Just remember they are also on a journey; be quick to forgive and bless them. If you commit yourself to share your life with others, they will soon become the net that helps you continue to tread water, and eventually get those sails full of the breath of God again. I have made a habit of surrounding myself with other believers so they can help validate my choices and direction I am heading on the journey.

How can you tell if the group you are part of will be helpful? Look at the fruit in their lives. Do they have peace, are they kind, do they have the respect of others, and do they have stories to share of God's faithfulness? If the answer is yes, those are the people you want in your boat!

## *Worship and thank God*

I know the last possible thing we feel like doing when we have hit rock bottom is praising God. Praise naturally comes out of a heart full of joy. If we are suffering, it can feel impossible to open our mouths to praise. However, more than any other activity, I have found that cranking some worship music and singing and dancing my heart out changes the atmosphere and changes my attitude. When I am at my lowest, I resist worship so strongly, but once I am reminded of the power it has to invite the Holy Spirit to intervene in my circumstance, it is easy to open my mouth and sing.

**Psalm 100: 1-5 (NIV) /**
**Shout for joy to the Lord, all the earth.**
**Worship the Lord with gladness; come**
    **before him with joyful songs.**
**Know that the LORD is God. It is he who**
    **made us, and we are his; we are his**
    **people, the sheep of his pasture.**
**Enter his gates with thanksgiving and his**
    **courts with praise; give thanks to him**
    **and praise his name.**
**For the LORD is good and his love endures**
    **forever; his faithfulness continues**
    **through all generations.**

The storms of life are challenges that act as a crucible to our faith. A test of where we will place our trust, our efforts, and our energy. Practically we can prepare ourselves when we see the clouds gather by ensuring we are putting on the armor of God, leaning into His life-giving word, praying and praising.

The Bible has so many illustrations of people that endure a storm for a time, and then rise victorious. Paul in prison literally breaks his own bondage with praise and then saves the prison warden. Joseph was sold into slavery, falsely accused and imprisoned, Job lost it all, and Jesus was crucified, and yet all of them were redeemed by God's mighty hand and not just brought back to where they were before the storm, but exalted even higher.

Trust that if you are in a storm, God is believing that you will hold fast to Him, trust Him, and make it through stronger and more powerful than you were before the clouds rolled in.

# Section 5

# Celebrate

### CHAPTER 23

# *Praise*

Did you know that sailors sang songs? I'm sure you have heard a particularly chipper rendition of one in Disneyland or perhaps something from *Pirates of the Caribbean*? These songs of the sea are called sea shanties and are the work songs of a ship. According to Rob Ossian these songs helped to propel the ship:

> In the days when human muscles were the only power source available on a ship, the sea shanties served a practical purpose: the rhythm of the song served to synchronize the movements of the shipworkers as they toiled at repetitive tasks. They also served a social purpose: singing and listening to songs is pleasant; it alleviates boredom, and lightens the burden of hard work.
> –Rob Ossian[1]

Most of these songs had a call and response pattern to them, where one sailor would start the song and the rest of the crew would respond. A call and response exchange signifies that a crew is working toward a common goal. I believe this pattern is useful when we are hard at work trying to get to our God ordained destination. We hear the call of the Lord and are encouraged to go to work in achieving our goal.

However, sometimes we get bored or tired of floating along, or sometimes we grow weary of the time it takes to get to our destination. It is during these moments that we need to begin to sing and praise our Creator. Praise can change the rhythm in which we find ourselves. It can propel us forward, motivate us, and alleviate the hard work that we might find ourselves doing.

Oftentimes we must begin praising before we see the shoreline of our intended destination. I have been discouraged many times in my journey by the length of time it seems to take to arrive at the destination I felt called to. Praise, as I mentioned before, is shown multiple times in the Bible to be the agent of change that literally breaks chains and prison cells.

Maybe praise comes easily to you. Maybe you have never even tried to praise. Praise is not being able to sing worship songs with a pretty voice or with great style, like many of our worship leaders. Praise is a condition of our heart. It is having a willingness to lay down our selfishness, our pride, our need to be right, and our very need to feel important to honor our creator with all that we are. When we worship God we are exhibiting a reverence and admiration for our Creator. No matter whether your voice is one intended for the shower, I can guarantee if you open your mouth and cry out to the Lord it sounds like music to Him. I'm confident in stating that all those hearty sailors were not all beautiful singers, but I'm certain that Praise will change things in your life.

### Psalm 98: 4-6 (NIV) /
### Shout for joy to the Lord, all the earth,

**Burst into jubilant song with music;
Make music to the Lord with the harp,
With the harp and the sound of singing,
With trumpets and the blast of the ram's horn—
Shout for joy before the Lord, the King.**

I had the benefit of informal praise training from a young age, courtesy of my mother. Regardless of whether you have children, I challenge you to this experiment that worked like a charm on me as a young, angst-ridden teenager. When I was in an unusually deep funk, my mother would sing silly songs of praise like, "I've got that joy, joy, joy, joy down in my heart. . .WHERE??!!" That last word was shouted with so much joy you could hardly keep yourself from smiling.

Even if you cannot carry a tune in a bucket, all you need to do is swing from high notes to low notes in a positively annoying pattern, with a massive smile to do the trick.

My mom is like a joy ninja. She has experienced a lot of pain and loss, especially in relationships, but she always finds a way to see the fun in life. Sometimes we need to sing a silly song and highlight the things in life that make it worth living. In case you needed another song, this was one of my mom's favorites, and ultimately became one of my own:

> Don't let the darkness get you down
> Rise up and take your holy crown
> Boldly walk in the light of day
> Don't let the darkness in your way

This particular song was a battle cry from my mom's heart that reminded me of who I was. I was a warrior princess and I was already standing on the side of the victory. She helped me recognize when I was believing the lies of the enemy, when I was defeated.

She highlighted the truth that I would not always feel depressed or inadequate, but that I was fearlessly and wonderfully made. I was God's glorious creation, made to conquer fear and made to carry the light of love and hope. Maybe that is why I know my mom will survive anything that comes her way. She tries to believe for the best, even when she feels her worst.

Let's challenge ourselves to be the same. When hope still seems far away or when you are on the very edge of giving up, I challenge you to blast your praise music and sing to the King of Kings. He is bigger than what you are facing and your voice is heard by Him during times of praise and thanksgiving. In your darkest hour, wouldn't you like to have the ear of the Creator of the Universe?

Sing out, dance with abandon, and trust that He will see His joyful son or daughter praising and hear the innermost cry of your heart. Let the tears flow, because trust me they will, when you really surrender yourself to praise. He will heal, release power, strengthen you, and give you courage for whatever you will face in this day and the next. Praise doesn't always come naturally; it is something that needs to be practiced. I am sure you have had days where you feel really depressed or full of shame and doubt and the last thing you want to do is celebrate.

This "feeling" keeps us from opening the door of our hearts and quite literally our mouths to praise. When I have encountered circumstances that were downright awful, my mouth felt bolted shut. I didn't want to praise God and frankly, sometimes, I felt angry with Him. There have been many times when I have been in church during worship but felt reluctant to join in. These emotions and feelings of rebellion are not helpful in moving us toward God's plan. We must develop a habit of compelling ourselves to praise when we are most vulnerable to depression, doubt, and fear.

I know that when my hands are heavy and my voice is weak, it's time to break free into praise.

**Psalm 63:4 (NIV) /**
**I will praise you as long as I live,**
**And in your name I will lift up my hands.**

Lift your hands toward heaven and give Jesus a little "touch-down" move. Or if you love to dance, move with praise in your bones. If you need a jumping off point, please see a recommendation below to start your praise party.

Below is a list of some of the names of God. Use this list to start praising, especially when you are struggling. Just speak them out loud, and then be prepared to jump into a song, because I can almost guarantee you will be ready to ROCK once you have read through this list a few times. In fact, if you can, why not do it now?

| | |
|---|---|
| King of Kings | Jesus my Refuge |
| Creator of the Universe | God of Heaven and Earth |
| Lord of Lords | God my Provider |
| Lion of Judah | Jesus my Healer |
| The Good Shepherd | Son of God |
| Prince of Peace | Jesus my Salvation |
| Jesus my Comforter | Jesus my Rock |
| Jesus my Counselor | Creator of the stars |
| Mighty God | Giver of every good thing |
| God my Protector | Jesus my Family |

If you are tired or weary of the journey, I want to encourage you no matter how challenging it feels, start to praise God. Praise Him not just for what He can do for you, but for who He is. Whether you feel His presence or can comprehend His greatness, praising your Creator will change you from the inside out. If you need endurance, praise Him. If you need healing, praise Him. If you need strength, praise Him. If you need courage, praise Him. If you need wisdom, praise Him. If you need joy, praise Him. If you need provision, praise Him. No matter what your need, He is already waiting for you to come to Him with praise and thanksgiving.

Just as the sailors used songs to move their ship along in a consistent rhythmic pattern, your praise will build forward momentum in your journey. The sailors of old used their sea shanties to lift the burden of heavy labor, in a like manner the act of praising will lift your burdens. It's never fun to think you are getting nowhere unless you are having a party while you are waiting for your somewhere! When in doubt, praise it out!

### CHAPTER 24

# Rest

Whether you can see your destination on the horizon or you are still out on the high seas, you will need to learn how to rest. Sailing crews would take shifts of rest and work. While one group was on watch, the others were resting. We need to observe shifts of rest and work as well. Our bodies and minds can only endure so much effort before things start to break down.

Have you been going through a season where you have forgotten what day of the week it is? Or you haven't had a vacation in a while, or maybe ever? You have been going a million miles an hour and you don't really know how to slow down?

If so, I understand you! This is one of the most difficult chapters for me to write because I struggle to rest. I try to do a lot of things in my own strength. I forget that my God is all powerful and His intentions were not for me to be in a constant state of striving.

When we feel as though we are unable to take time to rest ,we are not trusting in God. We are in a mindset of pride. This mindset causes us to believe that if WE don't do something than it won't get done, or things will fall apart. This is sinful and it separates us from the generous person of God. He determined the length of every day and mandated in his word there would be six days of work and one for rest. God set aside the Sabbath day as holy.

**Genesis 2:2 / By the seventh day God had finished the work he had been doing; so on the seventh day he rested from all his work (NIV)**

We shouldn't allow ourselves the margin to believe that we can accomplish more than God did without taking rest. If God took the time to look at the work he had accomplished and rested, we should do the same. Let's be intentional about honoring our shifts of rest and work.

There are two forms of rest I want to examine: supernatural rest and physical rest.

## *Supernatural Rest*

Supernatural rest is found in and through our work. It transcends our circumstances, no matter how crazy things might be. This type of rest is rooted in trusting God's way, God's plan, and the grace we are offered through Jesus. The following scripture was a promise given to us from Jesus:

**Matthew 11: 28-30 / Come to me, all who are weary and burdened, and I will give you rest. Take my yoke upon you, and learn from me, for I am gentle and humble in heart, and you will find rest for your souls. For my yoke is easy and my burden is light. (NIV)**

Jesus used a farming analogy to reveal to us how we find rest even as we carry heavy burdens. A yoke was placed across two oxen in order to share the burden of pulling the load. Farmers would pair an older ox with a younger one to teach them how to pull the load. The younger would learn by walking in step with the older.[1]

Jesus calls us to place His yoke upon us and walk in step with Him. As we trust Jesus and follow His example, the yoke we carry will become lighter. We will accomplish more because we are not relying on our own strength, but we are trusting in the strength of Jesus.

If we continue to work without trusting in the help and strength of Jesus, we will eventually wear out. Just like an ox who pushes ahead of their partner will stumble often, wear out more quickly, and ultimately delay the progress of the work. We too will stumble, endure pain, and delay our progress.

I remember a season of my life where I was living in an almost constant state of being stressed out and overwhelmed. It was during this season that I was in charge of our company's finance department. I was put in charge of the spreadsheets even though I had no formal training in bookkeeping, human resources, or accounting. I was completely out of my depth to do a good job.

Nonetheless, I wasn't about to quit, as I am probably one of the most head strong people you will ever meet. I sat in a tiny office day after day, trying to learn how to run profit and loss statements, calculate taxes, and manage our payables and receivables. It was grueling and even though I had help from a part-time bookkeeper, I was still drowning. I was onboarding the operations responsibility of our whole company onto myself, and I was overwhelmed.

I didn't trust anyone to help me figure it out.

After a few months of this ongoing personal saga, I sat with a friend of mine who asked me a simple question: "Do you feel God has called you to this work, in this season?"

I said, "Yes, even though I don't like it."

She chuckled and told me that I needed to lean on Jesus to help me learn how to do this role well. She reiterated what I already knew: don't try and do more than God has asked you to do. Trust in His plans and His methods.

Slowly but surely, when I finally surrendered to receive help from Jesus, I started to be more capable of taking each day with a step-by-step approach. I wasn't trying to "get it all done" so I could be done. This led to seeing more of Jesus working through my department to bring integrity, faith, and hope to the other teams. I was finding supernatural rest while I was working at the tasks God had set before me.

Supernatural rest is what we find as we work alongside Jesus. If you have pulled up anchor and you are on your journey, you will encounter situations where you struggle to find rest. These struggles will be an indication that you need to harness yourself to Jesus. Lean into the power and freedom He offers for your life. We are not meant to pull all the weight of our calling.

### Physical Rest

The other type of rest is the variety we often associate with the term "rest. It's physical rest and is more like relaxation, in the form of a good night's sleep or enjoying an unhurried and unscheduled day. The word Sabbath means sanctified, or set apart. We are to set apart a day out of each week in order to observe a day of rest. Our bodies and our minds need this kind of physical rest in order to reset and recharge.

When we experience long term stress our bodies start to wear out. People who have endured long term stress can suffer from heart disease, diabetes, obesity, asthma, anxiety and depression, among others. Ask yourself if whatever your chasing is worth suffering through these illnesses.

Perhaps during the journey, your survival mechanism took over and you didn't take time to eat properly or sleep enough because of the waves of stress you were navigating. You might be starting to see the warning symptoms that you have gone too long without rest. Hopefully during the storm you were still clinging to God's supernatural rest and peace, but you must take time to embrace physical rest!

The Bible says,

## "Be still and know that I am God." Psalm 46:10 (NIV)

I struggle with being still in any circumstance, especially when I am going through a very difficult season of life. I am usually antsy and feel like I have to do something to deserve peace and rest, as though I must earn stillness. Thankfully, God doesn't work that way. He commands us to BE STILL.

I liken this to when we hold a sleeping infant. When babies are restless and squirmy, we do everything we can to comfort them and settle them into rest. It is the most wonderful feeling to hold a sleeping child that is at peace. I think this is how Our Heavenly Father feels about us, when we are constantly wriggling. He wants us to rest our weary heads on His chest and be still, listening to the heartbeat of heaven. He wants to restore us and refresh our spirits.

So how do we practically observe Sabbath rest and make a habit of taking physical rest?

### *Get enough sleep*

Each person is different in the amount of sleep they require to feel their best. I feel most rested and ready for my day when I get between seven and eight hours of sleep. Alex can subsist on less than that, and typically only gets around six hours of sleep every night. My daughter is just like her dad, and my son is unlike any of us in that he can sleep for ten or more hours.

Regardless of how much sleep you require, it is important to attempt to get the minimum amount your body craves almost every night. If you have gone for a few days or weeks where you haven't gotten enough sleep, your body will be vulnerable to illness and disease.

### *Exercise*

I'm not talking about the anguishing type of exercise that pushes your body to the limit. I'm talking about moving each day in a way that gets your blood moving and is enjoyable. I love taking a walk outside or going for a hike. If you have bad joints, try going for a bike ride, swimming, or kayaking. Getting outdoors and moving around is good for the body and soul. But even if all you are able to do is stretch some, this can dramatically improve your overall body function.

Recently, I went golfing with Alex. It was the first time it was just the two of us, and it was one of the most wonderful days of rest. We weren't bombarded by the chores of our home or by the constant beeping of our phones. We spent a whole afternoon walking a beautiful course and attempting to knock a tiny white ball toward an exceptionally small hole. I am rubbish at golf. However, I don't let my scores or my skills prevent me from getting out there and enjoying a day of light exercise.

I encourage you to find something you can do that gets you moving. Don't judge yourself, just try out a few things until you find an activity that feels restful to you.

## Schedule an unscheduled day

The Sabbath was a day that was set apart. According to the laws found in the Old Testament, it was a day where the Jewish people were not supposed to do their ordinary work. That didn't mean they did nothing, but it did mean that Mom got a break from cooking and Dad got a break from carpentry.

I have to protect our Sabbath days. I keep the calendar for our house and we try to observe the Sabbath on Saturdays because it tends to be the day that is consistently open. This means that we try not to make any plans for the day that relate to our regular weekly activities. Work is set aside and we plan family activities. This doesn't happen on its own. I must plan for the unplanned day. Otherwise, a million different things will find themselves on our calendar.

The point of the Sabbath is to give yourself time and space to breathe, to take a break from your everyday, and to be still. I have found that on these precious days I find joy again. I find peace in the unhurried pace. I find that the worries of my week seem less prominent. I want to encourage you to find one day out of every week where you can enjoy an unscheduled day. Protect this day! Even though it will be challenging, it will be worth it.

## Give your worries to God

Taking time to rest requires faith. We are consumed with worries. How we are going to make our mortgage payment? Who is going to fix our washing machine? What school are the kids going to attend? How are we going to pay for that school? Who am I going to marry? Am I going to get married?

We are reluctant to take a day of rest or a moment of rest because we are constantly assaulted by the cares of this world.

Let me ask you, if your dad was the President, would you worry about having a place to live, or food to eat, or having a job? Would you worry if you were in big trouble? Wouldn't you be confident that your dad would take care of you? Not only would you worry less, but you would have expectations that good things would come to you.

It's no secret that doors open for children of highly influential, powerful, and successful parents. How much more resources, patience, compassion, and willingness to provide is our Heavenly Father? If you are a follower of Jesus, remind yourself of who your dad is. He is the "president" of it all. Give him all of your concerns, and trust that He will take care of you. God loves us so much, we cannot even comprehend the depths of His compassion. Take the time to relax and restore in the very capable arms of your Heavenly Father.

As you journey, you will need to take shifts of rest and work. As you work, remind yourself that Jesus is right beside you, ready to help you shoulder the weight of your destiny. Set aside time each week to be restored by doing things out of your ordinary work week. And finally, take good care of your body with good sleep, gentle exercise, and releasing your worries to God. Observing rest throughout your journey will help you find many safe harbors along the way.

### CHAPTER 25

# *Safe Harbor*

As you progress toward safe harbor, you can finally see the shoreline of the place that you have longed to see. How good this must have felt to sailors that spent months traveling the open water. Finally, a place to put down anchor and take a break for a moment. Can you imagine living at sea for months or years at a time and then finally landing at the intended destination? I would likely hit the ground and fall on my face kissing it over and over again. I would breathe it all in and rejoice in the fact that I was no longer floating. What does it mean for you to find safe harbor? The definition of safe harbor according to the Collins Dictionary[1] is as follows:

1.  A place that offers protection from the weather, attack, etc.
2.  A refuge or break from suffering
3.  something that protects and allows something to flourish

It is a place of protection, a shelter from the storm; it is a place that allows enough time, strength, and resources to flourish. I know that many of us, when we set out on a journey with God, have a vision of what it will look like in the end. During the course of that journey, the end can oftentimes look very different from what we expected. The journey, the storms, and the challenges are meant to change us for the better. They make us stronger, they test and increase our faith, and they help us to understand the goodness of our Creator. What we started out thinking was our safe harbor may no longer be true.

Regardless, you should feel a deep sense of peace that this particular season is coming to a close or, at the very least, a nice pause. You can sense that you are in a place where you can begin to regroup.

When I got engaged to Alex, I found peace. I had come out of a long season of uncertainty in the area of relationships and when I said "yes" to a beautiful ring on my finger, I knew this was going to be a place of rest and healing for me. We were engaged for only eight months and during that time I felt joy, peace, and excitement for the future. The old insecurities of my past began to fall away. The storms of failed relationships were clearing, and God was breaking through the clouds to show me His destiny for my life. My marriage hasn't been all sunshine and rainbows, but during that moment of my journey, I had found a safe harbor.

As you come into your own safe harbor, I strongly urge you to write down the details of God's faithfulness through the adventure. While you are in a place of strength and solidarity it is good to commit the story and it's details to memory. I don't know how you personally do this, but there are many ways to commemorate coming into safe harbor. Depending on where God has led you, it might consist of writing down the story in a journal, or throwing a party to celebrate; it could also be planting something that will grow or donating to a good cause.

Be intentional about how you come into your safe harbor. Create a lasting memory so that as you continue on your journey you will be reminded of your victory and God's faithfulness to pull you through.

### CHAPTER 26

# *Final Destination*

"The wind in her sails" is the phrase that made me consider what it meant to chart a course. What does it mean to make a plan with God at the helm? For me it is summed up in one of my favorite scriptures:

> **Proverbs 3:5-6 / Trust in the Lord with all your heart and lean not on your own understanding; in all your ways submit to Him, and He will make your paths straight. (NIV)**

Charting a course with God at the helm requires faith, a deep trust in the person and goodness of God. Choosing God as your captain signifies that you acknowledge you need His help to reach your destination. When you make plans and you submit them to the Lord, He will ensure safe passage. Even though you will encounter rough seas, days where you feel lost, and possibly get shipwrecked, God promises never to abandon you. He will be out in the middle of the ocean with you and He won't leave you to drown.

Be prepared for shifts in circumstances and changes in the wind. These are opportunities to trust even more deeply. Keep your eyes firmly focused on God, look to see what your captain is doing, and follow His lead. Read your Bible, set aside time to recalibrate your ears to hear the Holy Spirit, seek out counsel from others, and praise God even when you don't feel like it. Your responsiveness will make a difference in how long and painful stormy seasons may seem. Don't distress when you run aground and your world seems to fall apart. While God doesn't intentionally inflict suffering, He is faithful to teach us how to rebuild. He will restore what was broken and lost. I have full confidence in saying this because I know my final destination. It is a place where all that is wrong is made right, all that was sorrowful turns to joy, and death loses its power.

As a follower of Jesus, my final map dot is Heaven. It is the place I continue to journey toward as I follow God's lead in my life. When I finally arrive, all the tears will be wiped away. I will understand the character of God because I will be able to commune with Him eternally. While I look forward to that day, I'm not quite there yet.

God has placed a desire within me to encourage those around me to share in the same final destination. This is why I must continue to encourage myself to explore the unknown. I must do things I never thought possible. I must befriend people I wouldn't normally choose. I must build a crew of loving and wise people who will help me persevere through the difficult times. I must trust in God's plan more than I trust in my circumstances.

Part of my journey has obliged me to write this book, but this is only part of the adventure God has called me to. My chart has already had many stops, but there are many more to go. As I continue to explore the high seas, I am learning more and more about what it means to follow Jesus; to love more, to serve more, and to live a full life of adventure. I'm hoping one day Jesus might actually teach me to walk on water!

Do you have a good idea where God is calling you to go? Have you pulled up anchor and are already out to sea? Do you feel like you are stuck on an island of uncertainty? Perhaps you are just beginning to explore what it means to let God lead? Let me reassure you, God is aware of your precise location. He is ready to lead and guide you back to himself and the safe harbor of His love.

When we chart a course with God at the helm, we select a final destination that is worthy of the adventure. We make plans according to God-appointed dreams and goals. We prepare ourselves through intimate relationship with the Holy Spirit, trust in God's ability to provide, and we endure all of the setbacks we encounter. We praise even when we cannot see the end. Because when we submit our journey to God as our captain, we'll continue to travel toward our final safe harbor, the harbor of Heaven.

I pray that you will be courageous enough to embark on the journey God has designed, that you would have the audacity to believe in supernatural dreams, and that you have the stamina to see it through to its glorious end.

### PLAN • PREPARE • PERSEVERE • PRAISE

# NOTES

## Preface

1. *Seatalk, The Dictionary of English Nautical Language*, www.seatalk.info, keyword (Chart a Course), published by Mike MacKenzie, Nova Scotia, 2005.

## Introduction

1. THE HOLY BIBLE, NEW INTERNATIONAL VERSION®, NIV® Copyright © 1973, 1978, 1984, 2011 by Biblica, Inc.® (All subsequent NIV references are from this source)

## Chapter 1

1. "Chart No. 1 United States of America Nautical Charts and Symbols Abbreviations and Terms." www.seasources.net, www.seasources.net/PDF/ChartNo1.pdf.

## Chapter 3

1. "course line." *McGraw-Hill Dictionary of Scientific & Technical Terms, 6E*. 2003. The McGraw-Hill Companies, Inc. 30 Jul. 2019 https://encyclopedia2.thefreedictionary.com/course+line

## Chapter 4

1. O'Connor, O. and Robertson, E. (2009). *Levi ben Gerson* (1288-1344). [online] www-history.mcs.st-andrews.ac.uk. Available at: https://www-history.mcs.st-andrews.ac.uk/Biographies/Levi.html [Accessed 13 Sep. 2019].

2. "File:Fotothek df tg 0003339 Geometrie ^ Vermessung ^ Instrument. jpg." Wikimedia Commons, the free media repository. 31 Oct 2018, 09:33 UTC. 30 Jul 2019, 19:38 <https://commons.wikimedia.org/w/index.php?title=File:Fotothek_df_tg_0003339_Geometrie_%5E_Vermessung_%5E_Instrument.jpg&oldid=325985617>.

**Chapter 5**

1. "About." *Sully Sullenberger,* Aug. 2012, http://www.sullysullenberger.com/about/.

2. *Holy Bible: English Standard Version.* ESV Crossway Bibles, 2001. (All subsequent ESV references are from this source)

**Chapter 6**

1. Holy Bible: New Life Version: with Topical Study Outlines. Barbour Bibles, an Imprint of Barbour Publishing, Inc., 2003, www.biblegateway.com/passage/?search=2 Corinthians 10: 5 &version=NLV. (All subsequent NLV references are from this source)

2. Reigler, F. (n.d.). .

3. Achor, Shawn. *The Happiness Advantage: the Seven Principles That Fuel Success and Performance at Work.* Virgin, 2011.

4. Fredrickson, Barbara L. "The role of positive emotions in positive psychology: The broaden-and-build theory of positive emotions." *American psychologist* 56.3 (2001): 218.

**Chapter 7**

1. Twitter, 25 June 2016, twitter.com/sugarrayleonard/status/746802609411993600, Sugar Ray Leonard "Your dreams are your GPS to your success so Never stop dreaming"

2. *Holy Bible: New Living Translation.* Tyndale House Publishers, 2015. (All subsequent NLT references are from this source)

3. Johnson-Sirleaf, Ellen. *This Child Will Be Great: Memoir of a Remarkable Life by Africas First Woman President.* Harper, 2009.

**Chapter 8**

1. Welch, Catrina. "9 Ways God Is like a GPS." Catrina Welch, Author, Speaker, 9 Aug. 2014, catrinawelch.com/9-ways-god-is-like-a-gps/.

**Chapter 9**

1. Wikipedia contributors. "Compass rose." Wikipedia, The Free Encyclopedia. Wikipedia, The Free Encyclopedia, 30 Jul. 2019. Web. 30 Jul. 2019.

2. "Dead Reckoning." *Merriam-Webster,* Merriam-Webster, https://www.merriam-webster.com/dictionary/dead reckoning.

### Chapter 13

1. Chambers, Oswald. *My Utmost for His Highest Devotional Journal*. Edited by James Reimann, Discovery House, 1992.

### Chapter 14

1. "Persevere: Definition of Persevere in English by Lexico Dictionaries." *Lexico Dictionaries | English*, Lexico Dictionaries, www.lexico.com/en/definition/persevere.

2. Meyer, Joyce. "Testimony Begins with Test: Daily Devo." Joyce Meyer Ministries, 29 May 2018, joycemeyer.org/dailydevo/2018/05/0529-testimony-begins-with-test. Adapted from the resource *Trusting God Day by Day Devotional* - by Joyce Meyer

3. Walter Mischel, Ozlem Ayduk, Marc G. Berman, B. J. Casey, Ian H. Gotlib, John Jonides, Ethan Kross, Theresa Teslovich, Nicole L. Wilson, Vivian Zayas, Yuichi Shoda, 'Willpower' over the life span: decomposing self-regulation, *Social Cognitive and Affective Neuroscience*, Volume 6, Issue 2, April 2011, Pages 252–256, https://doi.org/10.1093/scan/nsq081

4. "Headwind: Definition of Headwind in English by Lexico Dictionaries." *Lexico Dictionaries | English*, Lexico Dictionaries, www.lexico.com/en/definition/headwind.

### Chapter 18

1. *The Holy Bible: Containing the Old and New Testaments*. Thomas Nelson, 2018. NKJV 1982 (All subsequent NKJV references are from this source)

### Chapter 19

1. MacKenzie, Earl. "What To Do When You Run Aground." *Cruising World*, 14 Feb. 2014, www.cruisingworld.com/how/what-do-when-you-run-aground/.

### Chapter 20

1. Cronin, Carol. "How To Sail Safely through a Storm." *North Sails*, North Sails, 16 Jan. 2018, www.northsails.com/sailing/en/2016/09/how-to-sail-safely-through-a-storm.

2. "weathering the storm." *Farlex Dictionary of Idioms*. 2015. Farlex, Inc 30 Jul. 2019 https://idioms.thefreedictionary.com/weathering+the+storm

### Chapter 22

1. Sa'di, Muslih-Uddin. *The Gulistan or Rose Garden of Sa'di*. Lulu.com, 2008. Adapted quote "I complained that I had no shoes until I met a man who had no feet."

**Chapter 23**

1.  Ossian, Rob, and Rob Ossian. "What Is a Sea Shanty?" *History of Sea Shanties*, www.thepirateking.com/music/shanty_types.htm.

**Chapter 24**

1.  Weems, Kerri. "A Yoke for Rest?" *FaithGateway*, 2 Nov. 2017, www.faith-gateway.com/yoke-rest-jesus/#.XTniNJNKg0o.

**Chapter 25**

1.  "Safe Harbour Definition and Meaning: Collins English Dictionary." *Safe Harbour Definition and Meaning | Collins English Dictionary*, Harper Collins, www.collinsdictionary.com/us/dictionary/english/safe-harbour.

Made in the USA
Middletown, DE
09 October 2020

21535998R00104